PRAYERS
for
DIFFICULT
TIMES

When You Don't Know What to Pray

Men's Edition

Published by Barbour Books, an imprint of Barbour Publishing, Inc., 1810 Barbour Drive, Uhrichsville, Ohio 44683, www.barbourbooks.com

Our mission is to inspire the world with the life-changing message of the Bible.

Member of the
Evangelical Christian
Publishers Association

Printed in China.

PRAYERS
for
DIFFICULT
TIMES

When You Don't Know What to Pray

Men's Edition

Quentin Guy

BARBOUR BOOKS
An Imprint of Barbour Publishing, Inc.

CONTENTS

INTRODUCTION

*Don't bargain with God. Be direct. Ask for what
you need. This isn't a cat-and-mouse, hide-and-seek game
we're in. If your child asks for bread, do you trick him with saw-
dust? If he asks for fish, do you scare him with a live snake on
his plate? As bad as you are, you wouldn't think of such a thing.
You're at least decent to your own children. So don't you think
the God who conceived you in love will be even better?*

MATTHEW 7:7–11 MSG

• • •

Men tend to set prayer aside. We come to it as a last resort,
as that one power tool left that might do the job after we've
exhausted not only all other options, but ourselves. We know
we should pray more, and we know that the Bible shows Jesus
praying often as an example. We also know that many great
saints we admire prayed relentlessly. Yet we wait. That's the
crazy part. But the cool part is that God will always be there
to listen, whether we're crying out from a foxhole or seeking
Him daily.

No matter when you pray, or how often, remember that you
belong to God. He is your Father, God Almighty, your Lord, and
He is *for* you. So when hard times come, know for a fact that He
has allowed them. You may never know all the reasons He has
allowed a particular test, but that's where faith comes in. Will

7

you believe that He has His purposes for your difficulties? He can work out His will in and through the worst of times, so your choice is simple. Will you plug into the source of your power? Will you seek Him the way He told you to—by asking, seeking, and knocking *in prayer*?

Life has backed you into a corner in some way; whether you want to come out swinging or you've had the air knocked out of you, your best response is to go to God. "Cast your cares on the LORD and he will sustain you; he will never let the righteous be shaken" (Psalm 55:22 NIV).

This book covers various trials and tribulations many believers face. Use it to remind yourself that God is waiting to hear from you and that He is always with you in all situations. For each topic, you'll find verses and prompts to get you started. Many prayers can be adjusted to fit the needs of the person for whom you're praying.

This book can help you find some of the words you may need when you pray. But even more importantly, it can remind you whom you're talking to. Seek Him wholeheartedly and let Him work in your life. This is God's heart for you: "Because he holds fast to me in love, I will deliver him; I will protect him, because he knows my name. When he calls to me, I will answer him; I will be with him in trouble; I will rescue him and honor him. With long life I will satisfy him and show him my salvation" (Psalm 91:14–16 ESV).

ABUSE

"The thief comes only to steal and kill and destroy.
I came that they may have life and have it abundantly."

John 10:10 esv

• • •

Abuse is devastating in its complexity. It is often rooted in the shame and anger the abuser has suffered in his own life. Without realizing it, he spreads the poison to those closest to him, particularly his wife and kids. It's hard to admit for either party—the abuser and the one being abused—but it is so important to recognize the damage that's been done.

If you recognize yourself as an abuser and want to change, there's hope to be found in God. Abuse is a violation of trust, and trust takes time to rebuild once it's broken. You'll need God's light and strength to seek forgiveness and deal with the fallout of your behavior, but you'll also likely need pastoral and professional help to change your habits and restore your relationships.

Lord God, I am trying to face a fearful reality: I may be an abusive husband. It has been more than an occasional outburst of anger; it has become a pattern where I've tried to control my wife. It has led to harsh words and criticism of everything she does, even in public. I've threatened and isolated her and withheld my affection, support, and resources. I've failed the person You gave me to love and cherish. Help me rebuild what I've damaged, one day, one moment at a time.

• • •

Jesus, You have called me to be gentle and loving toward my wife: "Husbands, love your wives and never treat them harshly" (Colossians 3:19 NLT). I have not obeyed You. Help me to break from my negative thoughts and actions and to become more like You. Taken to extremes, my perfectionism becomes criticism, my jealousy becomes obsession, and my competitiveness becomes domination. Even though that's what I saw and experienced growing up, I know You have a better, higher way for me—to be merciful and humble, to treat my wife with respect and kindness.

• • •

Father, Your Word says that I am to love my wife "as Christ loved the church and gave himself up for her" (Ephesians 5:25 NIV). But even though I am a Christian, I am not Christ. I'm forgiven but still capable of falling—and that's what I've done with my wife. I've been harsh, unforgiving, and merciless with her. I am ashamed. I want to run, to ignore the problem, to shift the blame—but I can't. The way I treated my wife is my fault, no matter what she's done. Please forgive me and give me the courage to seek both her forgiveness and accountability from a church leader.

Jesus, my old abusive habits are tempting me today. Fill me with Your Spirit so that I won't belittle or criticize my wife or my children but build them up instead. Bring to mind what it looks like to be near me when I act badly—not so that I get stuck in the past, but so I can remember the cost of my sin. I am sick over what I've done, and it still nags at me. Help me, Lord, to make that extra effort to be loving and kind, even if I need to isolate myself until I am under control again. Let me live with my wife "in an understanding way" (1 Peter 3:7 ESV), and let me nourish and cherish her the way You nourish and cherish the church (Ephesians 5:28–29). Help me to guide my children "in the training and instruction of the Lord" (Ephesians 6:4 NIV) and to avoid exasperating them and "provoke[ing] them to wrath" (v. 4 NKJV).

• • •

Father, my wife is dealing with the effects of someone else's abuse. Help me to make our relationship a secure place, and empower me to avoid reacting to her stress and anger with my own. Even though I am surprised and heartbroken to find this out, help me to look past my own shock and seize the opportunity to begin to heal. I want to be like Joseph, who didn't understand the situation with Mary but still let his compassion and love for her guide his behavior toward her. Please heal my wife, and let me be part of that healing—especially when it's difficult, when it impacts our sex life and our friendship. I want to take the long view and trust You with the daily details.

ACCIDENTS

When I walk into the thick of trouble, keep me alive in the angry turmoil. With one hand strike my foes, with your other hand save me. Finish what you started in me, God. Your love is eternal—don't quit on me now.

PSALM 138:7–8 MSG

• • •

You didn't get out of bed this morning thinking, *I'm going to get in a car crash today*, or *Guess I'll break my arm at work*. There's a reason those kinds of incidents are called accidents. Not being able to anticipate them can make you feel helpless and frustrated, whether they happen to you or to someone close to you. But one thing an accident will never do is catch God off guard. His purposes are so unshakeable that He can bring something useful out of even the most unanticipated incident. So, rather than asking Him why an accident happened, ask for quick and complete healing and concentrate on what He wants you to get out of it.

Lord God, what happened makes me feel foolish and frustrated. Please give me Your perspective on the situation. Even if I can't see past my own part in the accident or understand why You let it happen, You can help me keep my focus on You. I trust that You can make something good come out of this annoying setback.

• • •

Father, this accident has turned my life upside down. It helps me understand what David meant when he wrote about not being able to sleep at night because of his anxiety. Like him, "I am weary with my groaning" (Psalm 6:6 NKJV). And like David, I ask, "O LORD, heal me, for my bones are troubled. My soul also is greatly troubled" (vv. 2–3). Deliver me from this, and help me to trust, as David did, that "the LORD will receive my prayer" (v. 9).

• • •

Father, my guilt over my part in this accident is eating me up. Others have suffered because of something I did. It doesn't help that I didn't mean for it to happen either. Forgive me, and comfort those this incident affects. Please help me figure out what to do— if I should make restitution or work toward restoring relationships, I'm willing. If I should just wait for a while and let things play out, help me to do that too. I trust Your timing, Your sovereignty, and that You can make good come out of bad.

• • •

God, You are perfect in all Your ways (Psalm 18:30). You are blameless and Your Word is tried and true. You are my shield and my refuge. Your timing is always just right. Help me keep my eyes on You. Make something good come out of this hot mess. This is who You are, and this is what You do.

ADDICTION

*Therefore submit to God. Resist the devil and he will
flee from you. Draw near to God and He will draw
near to you. Cleanse your hands, you sinners;
and purify your hearts, you double-minded.*

JAMES 4:7–8 NKJV

• • •

Addiction is a mask worn to cover up a deeper need. When
you're an addict, every puff of smoke, every needle prick, every
sip, every roll of the dice, every click alone in a dark room is a
search for something—escape, affirmation, purpose, success,
love. Here's the thing, though: God wants all of those for you.
He wants you to escape the enemy's lies and sin's bonds. He
affirmed your value in offering His Son—His very best—for you.
When you define purpose, success, and love through His eyes,
you clearly see the counterfeits of the world, the flesh, and
the devil for what they are. You also see the walls of the prison
you've built for yourself, and if you really want out, Jesus came
to set you free (Luke 4:17–21).

*I'm done with the lies I've been telling myself and others,
Father. I see my addiction for what it is—a false face I've tried to
put on to deal with my problems. I want to see Your face, and I
want to live my whole life like You are right here next to me.
I commit myself to living in integrity before You—to consistently
walking in a pattern of thoughts, words, and deeds that bring
true life. . .and open my heart to You. Thank You for loving
me even though You know what I have been and done.*

• • •

*Lord God, I've sacrificed so much to my addiction—time,
resources, relationships. Help me to be a "living sacrifice"
(Romans 12:1 NIV) so I can redeem all those things. Fill
me with Your Spirit, make Your Word come alive for me,
and help me to find godly counsel and accountability.
You are for me, God, so who can be against me? I need
You and desperately want to be on Your side.*

• • •

*God, I feel my addiction pulling on me today. Right now,
I want so badly to do the thing I used to do that I can't even think
straight. Help me to remember You. Bring Your Word to mind.
You said that "the one who endures to the end will be saved"
(Matthew 24:13 ESV). You are my goal and my reward. I know I need
endurance, so that when I have done Your will, I may receive Your
reward (Hebrews 10:36). "We are not of those who shrink back
and are destroyed, but of those who have faith and preserve
their souls" (v. 39 ESV). Pull me toward You.*

Jesus, set me free, so that I "will be free indeed" (John 8:36 NIV).
Like Paul, I don't understand why I do what I'm doing or why it's
so hard to do the right thing (Romans 7:15–24). I don't want to be
double-minded—trying to get both what You want and what I want.
What I do know is that I can't overcome my addiction—
but You can. I want to be patient, just like You are with me,
and committed to obeying You. I will seek You each day—
each moment, if necessary—from now on.

• • •

Father, cut me off from the things that tempt me, and from
the means I use to fulfill them—suppliers, resources, the internet,
social media, bad company. When I slip and fall, help me get
back up and try again. Because my sin hurts me, I know that
Your Spirit is working in me. You won't give up on me, but
please help me not to give up on myself. I know You
will deliver me through Jesus Christ.

ADULTERY

Adultery is a brainless act, soul-destroying,
self-destructive; expect a bloody nose, a black eye,
and a reputation ruined for good.
PROVERBS 6:32–33 MSG

• • •

Adultery cuts deep because it strikes not just at the heart of marriage but at the intimacy Christ desires with all Christians. The whole concept of becoming "one flesh" (Genesis 2:24 NIV) "is a great mystery, but I speak concerning Christ and the church" (Ephesians 5:32 NKJV). Jesus spoke of man not separating what God had joined together in the covenant of marriage (Matthew 19:6). Paul wrote, "He who loves his wife loves himself" (Ephesians 5:28 NKJV).

So, breaking that lifelong commitment to your spouse also breaks a promise to God, and it damages you too. Once you're joined to someone in marriage, you are unified in God's eyes into a whole greater than its parts. Adultery damages the unique intimacy of marriage, but God can repair it. However, the affair likely didn't happen overnight, so healing your marriage will take time—along with trust, transparency, and tenacity.

Father, I see my unfaithfulness for what it truly is—sin.
And first and foremost, I've sinned against You. Forgive me for
all the excuses I've made to justify my behavior. Nothing my wife
has done justifies my actions. The thought of confessing to her my
unfaithfulness terrifies me, but I understand that I need to do it. I
also understand that she is biblically justified if she chooses to
end our marriage. Give me the courage to do what is right—
and to continue to do what is right from now on.
Please save our marriage.

• • •

Lord God, right now I hurt so bad I can barely breathe. I know
I need to love my wife the way You love me—sacrificially, in spite
of my sin—but all I can think about is her sin. Forgive me for my
thoughts of what I'd like to do to the guy she cheated with. I know
vengeance is Yours, not mine (Hebrews 10:30). I don't know if I can
forgive her without Your help, but I know it's what You want me to
do. Calm the whirling of my thoughts and the churning of my gut.
Give me Your heart, Lord, because mine is broken.

• • •

Father, even though I'm heartbroken at what my wife has done, I
know I haven't been perfect. You told us to forgive others because
You've forgiven us (Ephesians 4:32), and You tell us to "make
allowance for each other's faults" (Colossians 3:13 NLT). As we go
through counseling and learn to live with each other in light of
what's happened, let Your love and grace flow through me. I need
Your peace desperately, through all the ups and downs.

God, I opened the door to something that turned me against my wife—bitterness or lust or emotional absence—and I poisoned my heart. I haven't yet acted on it physically, but I have indulged the thought of cheating. You've made it clear that I've already been unfaithful to her (Matthew 5:27–28), and I need to confess my sin to her. I need Your strength to do that, and I need Your Spirit to help me find the words and to receive her reaction. Help me to make "a covenant with my eyes" (Job 31:1 NIV). I commit to staying true to my wife, to breaking contact with the sources of my temptation—the other woman, social media, second looks, flirting at work, looking at porn—whatever I need to do to heal our hearts and our marriage.

• • •

God, I've been unfaithful to my wife. I've told her, and we are getting help to deal with the pain I've caused. We both have things to work on. Strengthen us to love each other, to show grace, to forgive, and to keep our hearts set on You. Heal our relationship.

ALCOHOL ABUSE

As a prisoner for the Lord, then, I urge you to
live a life worthy of the calling you have received.

EPHESIANS 4:1 NIV

• • •

Whatever drives your drinking—a rough upbringing, emotional or physical suffering, wanting to fit in or stand out—be certain alcohol abuse is not God's best for you. If you think you have a problem with drinking, you're probably right.

You've probably had those mornings when you woke up feeling like the dog's dinner, not remembering where you've been or who you were with—or worse, remembering all the excruciating details of your out-of-control behavior. You are being reckless with a life that is meant to honor God. He has good plans for you (Jeremiah 29:11), and He wants you to live a full, exciting life. You bear His image, which means you are an eternal being with whom He wants a close relationship.

Alcoholism makes it impossible to have healthy, trusting relationships with people, not to mention your Creator, but God can help you turn it around—if you're serious about giving it up.

Jesus, give me the courage to seek help. I've hit rock bottom many times, and it's clear to me that I can't quit drinking on my own. I need Your help, but I also need accountability—strong Christian men who can support and encourage me to switch my dependency over to You. I feel like I need to relearn how to live without alcohol. Fill me with Your Spirit and make me hungry for Your Word. Teach me how to die to myself and follow You.

• • •

Father, I've fallen again. I lied to myself, telling myself that one little drink wouldn't hurt. But I don't drink to do anything but get drunk, and I can feel the distance it creates between You and me. I hate it, and I'm fighting not to hate myself. Remind me of Your love—and that You died for me while I was still a sinner (Romans 5:8). You know what I am, but You still see me as worth the cost of Your only begotten Son to redeem. I don't understand that kind of love, but I want it desperately. Forgive me, and help me recommit to sobriety, right now.

Lord, I need Your wisdom and strength to avoid situations and people that compromise my commitment to follow You and stop drinking. Help me to recognize the triggers that push me to drink—the stress or exhaustion or whatever it may be. I want to learn to take care of myself, physically and spiritually, but I can't do it without You.

• • •

God, I want to bring my thoughts under Your control. I can make all kinds of arguments and excuses for why I drink, but I need to wage my war against alcoholism in the spiritual realm. As Your Word says, "For though we walk in the flesh, we do not war according to the flesh. For the weapons of our warfare are not carnal but mighty in God for pulling down strongholds, casting down arguments and every high thing that exalts itself against the knowledge of God, bringing every thought into captivity to the obedience of Christ" (2 Corinthians 10:3–5 NKJV).

ANGER

Whoever is slow to anger is better than the mighty,
and he who rules his spirit than he who takes a city.

PROVERBS 16:32 ESV

• • •

When we're angry, we often feel like an alternate personality has taken control. As we look back at times when we became angry—or even as it happens—it seems like we're watching an out-of-control lunatic who just happens to look a lot like us. What we're really watching, though, is our old self—our flesh—temporarily hijacking the new, spiritual man we are in Christ.

The threat is always there, and it always will be. . .until we die or until Jesus returns. So, it's necessary to learn how to understand and deal with your anger. Anger itself is not a sin; in fact, it's often a righteous response to injustice or sin—the very things the Bible shows us make God angry. It's all in how you respond to it. Do you grip your anger and channel it to constructive ends, or does it grip you and use you like a live-wire, causing shock and damage? You have a choice, because the Holy Spirit is in you and will guide and strengthen you to redirect your frustrations toward positive ends.

*Remind me, Father, that You have made me a new man in Christ.
I am a new creation (2 Corinthians 5:17), and You have redeemed
me from the curse of sin (Galatians 3:13). You will complete the
good work You started in me (Philippians 1:6), and I am Your
"workmanship, created in Christ Jesus for good works, which [You]
prepared beforehand that [I] should walk in them" (Ephesians 2:10
NKJV). Knowing these things, I can choose what to do when I get
angry. I can put that energy into making things right or addressing
injustice—and I don't have to lose my cool, because You are with me.*

• • •

*Lord God, I have let my anger control me. It's like I've let
a baby drive my car, and I understand that I'm not accomplishing
Your purposes when I blow my top (James 1:20). So many
things make me angry—disrespect, incompetence, selfishness,
messiness, lack of consideration—but abdicating my control
only makes them more likely to anger me. I need Your wisdom
to understand which offenses are real and which ones are only
perceived. And then, I need to let go of the perceived ones with
grace and forgiveness, and deal with the real ones with
respectful honesty, sympathy, and understanding.*

• • •

*Father, Your Word says, "Good sense makes one slow to anger,
and it is his glory to overlook an offense" (Proverbs 19:11 ESV).
I need to consider what it's like to be on the other side of me,
especially when I get angry. I don't respond well when people
get angry with me; why would they respond to my anger any
differently? I can assert myself and make the points I need to
make without losing my temper, but I need Your help to
increase my self-awareness and to respond humbly.*

God, it occurs to me that my anger is really an expression of pride. I thought I was setting someone straight, but I was really just putting myself in Your place. Forgive me. Only You know the whole story behind every situation. Only You know the full motives in each person's heart, including mine. I want to put others ahead of myself and their interests ahead of mine. You've made it clear that's what You want too: "In humility value others above yourselves, not looking to your own interests but each of you to the interests of others" (Philippians 2:3–4 NIV).

• • •

Father, I come from a long line of angry ancestors. I know what it is to go without kind words or physical affection. I've lived for so long without my father's blessing, and it has made me bitter and prone to angry words and actions. Give me Your blessing, Father, so that I can break this cycle and love my kids the way I should have been loved—the way You love me. May I teach them to love You and Your Word, and let laughter and honest, respectful conversation be the rule of my house.

ANXIETY

*And we know that God causes everything to work
together for the good of those who love God and
are called according to his purpose for them.*
<small>ROMANS 8:28 NLT</small>

• • •

You know the verse you just read; you've seen it over and over again. It'd be easy to blow it off—*Oh, yeah, Romans 8:28, sure, God's at work. . .whatever.* Please don't. Go back and read it again. Unpack it a bit. What does God cause to work together? *Everything.* Not *some* things, or *certain* things at certain times, but *all* things. To what purpose? *For the good.* God is good and He causes good to happen. For whose good? *Those who love God.*

Do you love God? Then this is for you. God's attention and power is focused on every detail of your life. And don't skip the last part of the verse: God has *called* you to live a good life of love with Him. It's His plan for you. God knows about whatever is stressing you out right now, and, believe this, His purposes for good are in it. Give your anxiety to Him and watch Him weave it into the tapestry of His amazing story and the special role you play in it.

I'm underwater, Lord, pressed down by weights I can't lift. All I want is to know what You want me to do, but it feels like I'm running out of air. I'm spending a lot of energy trying not to panic, and it's making me physically sick. I know what David meant when he said, "O Lord, heal me, for my bones are troubled. My soul also is greatly troubled; but You, O Lord—how long?" (Psalm 6:2–3 NKJV). Hear me, please—I need air! Give me Your Spirit now and help me to breathe again.

• • •

Father, I am stressed out. Remind me that I am not alone in my struggles. You are my shepherd, my light and salvation, my rock, and my refuge. I am also not alone among Your people. Even King David, a man after Your own heart, felt stressed. He said, "When I kept silent, my bones wasted away through my groaning all day long" (Psalm 32:3 ESV). He was honest about his anxiety. But he also said, "When I was desperate, I called out, and God got me out of a tight spot" (Psalm 34:6 MSG). Bring me someone I can talk with, someone who can calm me and give me Your advice and guidance.

God, I am trusting that praying will bring me peace. You said I shouldn't be anxious—about anything!—but instead, I should bring all my requests to You and thank You for all You've done. I'm counting on Your promise that when I do that, "the peace of God, which transcends all understanding, will guard your hearts and your minds in Christ Jesus" (Philippians 4:7 NIV). Thank You, God, for caring about the things I care about.

• • •

Lord God, I'm trying to think about birds and lilies, about how You care for them and how I mean more to You than they do, free and lovely as they are. I'm on the lookout for the new batch of mercies You said You give me each morning (Lamentations 3:22–23). As generous as You are, I'm going to need more than a baker's dozen. I'm holding onto my faith, but it feels like a fistful of sand. Don't let me slip through Your grasp today, Father. Guard my heart and mind with Your peace, grace, and love. I trust You. I trust You. I trust You.

ARGUMENTS

Avoiding a fight is a mark of honor;
only fools insist on quarreling.
PROVERBS 20:3 NLT

• • •

For the Christian, there's a right way to fight. When it comes to arguments, start by looking at your own motives. What was *really* at the heart of the conflict? Was it really about who's doing the dishes or how the church was going to spend certain funds, or was it something deeper? Frustration and anger often result in harsh words, but what was driving the tension? Are you actually angry at the person, or are you upset about something else? When you see another's splinter, check your own eye for a log (Luke 6:42).

However, even when you treat the other person with respect, you sometimes just have to agree to disagree. Paul and Barnabas parted company over John Mark in Acts 15, but each went on to do God's work. The challenge of any argument is to do it with love, trying to resolve the issue for the other person's highest good. If you approach it the same way, you'll reconcile and move forward in peace. If it doesn't work out, God will honor your commitment to keeping His priorities. Remember, He humbles those who exalt themselves and exalts those who humble themselves (Matthew 23:12).

Stick to solid ground—loving God and others as yourself.

Whether it's someone who is unsaved or a fellow Christian, your commitment to resolution and dignity can bring conviction and perspective on what matters most.

Lord, I'm in conflict with someone, and my anger and frustration are building. I want to check myself against Your Word, though. I think of Peter, who was so sure he was justified in his defense of Jesus in the garden that he cut a guy's ear off. But Jesus rebuked him because he wasn't thinking of God's ways but men's (Mark 8:33). I need Your perspective on this situation. Help me to do what's right in Your eyes.

* * *

God, over and over, Your Word speaks against "quarreling"—getting involved in arguments that come from fleshly desires. The children of Israel argued that You had led them into the wilderness to die—and You had: to themselves. They struggled with letting You provide everything they needed. I need to figure out this whole need vs. want thing. I want to honor You by seeking what others need above what I want. I don't have to argue to get what I want; I just need to trust You and You will provide.

Father, I'm trying to think of a time when I won someone over by using angry, harsh words during an argument. And I can't. I may have made my point, but I lost trust— and a chance to honor You. Forgive me for the times I've tried to defend myself or You unnecessarily, or put a principle ahead of a person, or self-righteousness ahead of relationship. Let my offenses be limited to the truth of the Gospel.

• • •

Lord, I need to bear in mind that it isn't my job but the Holy Spirit's to convict people of sin (John 16:8). Yes, the world is broken and full of sinners. Yes, Your righteous standard condemns all of us, and yes, the world will be judged. But I can know all of this and not let it lead to condemning, judgmental words. I came to Christ because Your Spirit did His work in me. When it comes to my words, remind me to give Him space to work in others' hearts too. Then I can stand for Your truth in a gracious and loving way, and maybe the Spirit will work through me instead of despite me.

• • •

God, my mind is swimming with all the points I want to make, with what I think this other person needs to hear. But it's all mixed up with my anger and frustration, and possibly my self-righteousness and judgmental thinking. Give me clarity and the ability to think before I speak. If I need to take some time to sort it out, help me to find solutions, not comebacks or ways to embarrass others. If it turns out there's a real issue, help me to address it in a direct and respectful way—to deal with the issue and not attack the person. Fill me with Your Spirit so I can represent You well.

BANKRUPTCY

And the God of all grace, who called you to his eternal glory
in Christ, after you have suffered a little while, will himself
restore you and make you strong, firm and steadfast.
1 PETER 5:10 NIV

. . .

Declaring bankruptcy may not carry the stigma it once did, but as Christians, we need to give careful consideration to some things before pursuing it as an option.

While you have a responsibility to take care of your family (1 Timothy 5:8)—even if it's just you—there's a right way to do it. When you've prayed about your finances, sought counsel, whittled your budget down to the basics, and tried in good faith to deal with your creditors, and you still can't take care of your family, bankruptcy may be your only option. But as a Christian, even if you declare bankruptcy, you should still take responsibility for your debt—whatever brought it on.

Sometimes, life forces hardship on you—death, divorce, extended unemployment—and sometimes, you've bitten off more than you can chew—more house, more car, more unsecured debt. Either way, learn from it. How you manage your resources is part of your witness for Christ. Seek His forgiveness for your part in your financial problems, give Him any guilt or shame you may be feeling, and move forward in faith, seeking to avoid similar trouble in the future.

Jesus, when I received You as Lord and Savior, You gave me a fresh start, a chance to break from my past and be the man You made me to be. Now that I've reached a point where I've decided that declaring bankruptcy is my best financial option, I ask You to give me a fresh start here too. Help me to put lessons I've learned into practice so that I never have to put myself and my family through this again.

• • •

Lord, I know I need to pay off my debts, and I know I've failed to do so. Some of this has been due to circumstances beyond my control, but when I've gotten desperate, I've tried to handle it myself—and gotten nowhere. I'm giving all of this over to You, God. You can make a way where there is no other. Lead me and teach me. Bring me wise counselors and forgive me for not seeking You sooner.

• • •

Father, I've been whistling past the graveyard long enough. I've pretended that my financial problems aren't that serious, that I can handle spending more than I make, that I must take on debt if I ever want anything. I see what I've built, and it's a prison, not a lifestyle. Bankruptcy isn't the problem; my attitude is. Guide me as I seek to learn about handling money in a way that honors You, and protect me and my family as we sort this out.

• • •

I ask You for mercy, Father. The burden is crushing me, affecting my health and my relationships. I confess it's because I've tried do things my way instead of Yours. Be with me and help me to make it right, to pursue bankruptcy only when I've exhausted all other options, and to heal the relationships I've hurt with family and friends.

BETRAYAL

My companion stretched out his hand against
his friends; he violated his covenant.
PSALM 55:20 ESV

· · ·

Betrayal is like being spat upon, kicked when you're down, and having your wounds salted all at once—but worse. You almost never see it coming, so it often feels like you've been blindsided by a rampaging rhino. And the closer you are to your Judas, the worse it feels.

No one likes feeling naked and exposed, vulnerable to attack, and it's hard not to become angry, vindictive, or embittered as a result of betrayal. It's not something you can just "get over"—at least, not without God's help. God will never betray you or abandon you. He's always got your back, especially when others have plunged a knife into it. Only God can give you the strength to recover, which starts with the ability to forgive. Forgiveness will cleanse you of your bitterness and rebuild your defenses. It can even help you pray for the person who has wronged you—just as Jesus taught us to pray for those who persecute us (Matthew 5:44).

*Lord God, even though I want to strike back at my betrayer, I'm
going to cry out to You instead. Your Word says, "Don't repay evil
for evil. Don't retaliate with insults when people insult you. Instead,
pay them back with a blessing. That is what God has called you
to do, and he will grant you his blessing" (1 Peter 3:9 NLT). I can't
do that without You, though, so I give You my anger and my fear.
Fill me with Your Spirit so I can turn my cheek and honor You, even
when it takes the form of honoring the person who has hurt me.*

• • •

*Jesus, even though I've been wronged, I want to respond like You
did when You were wronged. You are my example: You committed
no sin, and no deceit was found in Your mouth. When men hurled
insults at You, You didn't retaliate. When You suffered, You made
no threats. Instead You entrusted Yourself to Him who judges justly
(1 Peter 2:22–23 NIV). You are my Lord and my Savior, and even
though I feel the ache of betrayal in my gut, I choose to be like You.*

Father, I don't think of myself as someone who has enemies.
But it turns out I do—and it's someone I know and trusted.
I'm hurt and angry. But I also realize You're giving me a chance
to do something You did—love my enemy—and that You're also
giving me a chance to live without bitterness and grudge-holding.
I never thought I'd be grateful for something that hurts so
much, but I thank You, Lord God. Help me to obey You.

• • •

Father, even as the sting of betrayal pulses inside me, I remember
that I'm a citizen of a different realm—Your kingdom. As much as
my flesh is pushing me to dish up revenge, to plot the downfall
of my betrayer, I hold to the truth that because I'm Yours, I don't
have to respond with vengeance. In fact, You have a better (though
harder) way for me: "Don't hit back; discover beauty in everyone. If
you've got it in you, get along with everybody. Don't insist on getting
even; that's not for you to do. 'I'll do the judging,' says God. 'I'll take
care of it' " (Romans 12:17–19 MSG). Hold me up, Father, and protect
me. Remember that I chose You at this low moment and lift me up.

CHALLENGES

You will keep him in perfect peace, whose mind
is stayed on You, because he trusts in You.
ISAIAH 26:3 NKJV

• • •

The real challenge behind getting through any trial is letting go of your tendency to try to have it your way *and* God's way at the same time. The tendency as a man is either to John Henry your way through the mountain yourself (remember, legend has it that, in the end, J.H. died of exhaustion), or to avoid taking responsibility (blame-shifting, even onto God, is often easier than trusting His unseen purposes). James called that being "double-minded" (James 1:8), and instability will result.

At some point, you'll face a challenge that is too big for you. It won't matter how many notches you have in your belt— the Great Sink Leak of '98, the Christmas In-Law Compromise of 2011—God will allow something to happen that will force your hand on the big question: *am I the master of my fate or is God?* Even as a Christian, your flesh pulls you toward the former. But you must resist handling challenges in your own strength. Better to decide now that God's strength never fails, that His peace surpasses understanding, and that His grace is enough for you.

Lord, I want to see this obstacle through Your eyes, to trust that Your purposes are in it. Your Word says that the testing of my faith produces patience and that when I'm not sure what to do, I should ask You for wisdom and You'll give it to me (James 1:2–5). I want to jump in and fix this situation myself, but I admit that I don't know enough right now to act. Show me how and when to get involved, and remind me to seek Your purposes in this.

* * *

God, I feel overwhelmed. This problem is too big for me, and I need Your help. I know that nothing happens without You knowing, so let that be enough for me. You are my strength and my peace. Let me see You on the path ahead of me, even if it's just one step ahead.

* * *

Father, I confess that when I'm facing a trial, my tendency is to ask why You've let it happen instead of what You're doing in me by allowing it. I trust that You are sovereign, that You are good, and that You will strengthen my faith through this challenge if I'm open to You. I set aside my desire to know all the reasons why, and instead I choose to trust that Your grace is sufficient for me.

God, my fear is threatening to cut me off from You. I'm afraid of failing to overcome this obstacle, of missing Your purposes in it, of letting others down. I confess my fear; help my unbelief. You are my Rock and my Salvation. Even if the earth crumbles beneath me, I know You are with me. I will look forward to seeing what You accomplish in and through me as I face this.

• • •

Lord God, I confess that I was getting all fired up about taking on this challenge but failed to seek You. I know Your Word warns against boasting about tomorrow (James 4:13–16). I know enough of Your grace, mercy, and oversight that I should know better than to make plans without You. Thank You for prompting me by Your Spirit to seek You now. I ask for Your guidance and blessing on the challenge in front of me. Help me to achieve Your will as I face it.

CHRONIC ILLNESS

Yet what we suffer now is nothing compared to the glory he will reveal to us later.

ROMANS 8:18 NLT

• • •

Illness reminds us that we live in a fallen world—that we are subject to sin, decay, and death. When an illness lingers, especially when we know it probably won't go away, we must remind ourselves of other things, namely that sickness and suffering were never part of God's plan for the world, and that His plan of redemption includes our ultimate healing from all physical maladies.

When we think of what we or someone else is going through daily, it's not wrong to recognize that it's unfair. But assessing blame for the injustice of chronic illness—which for many falls back on God at some point—is neither helpful nor biblically correct. As Jesus pointed out when His disciples asked whose sin caused a man to be born blind, "You're asking the wrong question. You're looking for someone to blame. There is no such cause-effect here. Look instead for what God can do" (John 9:3 MSG).

Jesus, I realize that this sickness is part of what You came to redeem. You've made me a new man spiritually, and I know that when You return, You'll make me a new man physically as well. In the meantime, though, I'm sick, and it's not going away. And while I don't like it, I want to sit still and let You work. Father, I know that even as my body fails, I can become more like Jesus in seeking Your will, drinking from the cup You've given me, and trusting You to redeem this suffering.

● ● ●

Lord God, give me eyes to see You work through my illness. You have plans that go beyond my pain—plans for my family and friends, plans for my doctors and caregivers, plans to let me minister to those who are suffering the way I am. I hate being sick, but I love You for giving me a reason to hope and to endure with expectation. I'm waiting, Lord; make something good come out of this.

Father, I am watching someone I love suffer, and it is so hard. I've never felt so helpless, so unable to make a difference. Only You can make something good come out of this. All I can say is, "Here I am." If I can be of service, let me serve. If I can just be there, let me be there. Even as I ask You to heal the one I love, let me be Your hands and ears for them.

* * *

Father, let this sickness cultivate in me a wilderness mentality. Meet me in the midst of pain and side effects and endless appointments, all the points where my path intersects with others' paths, and let my belief in You impact those interactions. There is so much more to this life than my pain. I want to see my hope—like when Job focused on seeing his Redeemer in person (Job 19:25). You sustain me today and every day, and You make the difficulties of my journey count for something greater—Your kingdom. Glorify Yourself in my broken body. I rest in the fact that, one day, You will glorify mine.

CHRONIC PAIN

"This would be my comfort; I would even exult in pain unsparing, for I have not denied the words of the Holy One."

JOB 6:10 ESV

• • •

Suffering is a mystery we will never fully understand. Even when we trust that God is with us and that He has purposes in allowing suffering, walking with it day in and day out is never easy. We need the support of family, friends, other believers, and medical professionals. Most of all, though, we need to draw close to God. He alone can give your pain a greater purpose, make your misery a ministry. If you can listen past the blaring intensity of your pain, you will hear His voice calling you to join Him in a profound intimacy that only those who have truly suffered can know.

Jesus, I know You suffered too. I know You are with me and that
You will never leave me alone in my pain. Help me be more like
You in the way I handle it. I trust that You see every ache, every
jolt, every burning nerve, every ounce of agony—and You know
what it feels like. I want to know what it feels like to share in Your
suffering—to know that I can honor God with how I handle this.

* * *

Father, I am tired of hurting all the time. I admit that I wonder
why You haven't answered the prayers sent up for my healing.
I feel like David when he cried out to You, "What will you gain if I
die, if I sink into the grave? Can my dust praise you? Can it tell
of your faithfulness? Hear me, Lord, and have mercy on me.
Help me, O Lord" (Psalm 30:9–10 NLT). But then I think of Paul's
claim, "To live is Christ, and to die is gain" (Philippians 1:21 NKJV).
There are times when I feel like death would be a relief, but even
when I'm suffering, let me represent You well.

*God, I feel so alone in my pain. The emotions it causes are
harder to deal with than the physical aspect (which is no picnic
either). Strengthen me in my spirit, then, so I can better deal
with the signals my body is sending. Build hope in my heart
that I can be more like Jesus because of this. Teach me that
contentment in this life is always elusive, that I need to look
beyond my circumstances to see something eternal: the love
Jesus Christ demonstrated for You and for others. Thank You for
the fellowship I have with You in my suffering (Philippians 3:10).*

• • •

*Lord, I'm so done with the stiff upper lip approach to pain. I've
cut myself off from people because my suffering embarrasses
me—like I've done something bad and I don't want anyone to think
You're punishing me. I know that's not how You are. Forgive me for
my pride, for thinking I have to face this alone. Help me let people
in, trusting that You can use my pain as part of what You're doing
in their lives, and use them to lessen my loneliness and suffering.*

CHURCH DISCORD

*His purpose was to create in himself one new humanity
out of the two, thus making peace, and in one body to
reconcile both of them to God through the cross,
by which he put to death their hostility.*

EPHESIANS 2:15–16 NIV

• • •

The church is a family, with all the benefits and challenges of one. We're united by the blood and common cause of Christ, but we don't always love each other the way He told us to (John 13:34–35). Remember, we are sinners by nature and by choice, and the church is made up of redeemed sinners. God is working on us, but old habits are hard to break. That doesn't excuse unbiblical behavior; it just explains it.

God hates strife in His family, particularly "a false witness who breathes out lies, and one who sows discord among brothers" (Proverbs 6:19 ESV). We should find common ground in Jesus, for "he himself is our peace, who has made the two groups one and has destroyed the barrier, the dividing wall of hostility, by setting aside in his flesh the law with its commands and regulations" (Ephesians 2:14–15 NIV). Instead of finding reasons to disagree and quarrel, we should breathe out grace and defend gospel truth. As Jesus said, "Blessed *are* the peacemakers, for they shall be called sons of God" (Matthew 5:9 NKJV).

Father, I am so frustrated with what I see at church. We've forgotten that You made us to be in relationship with You and with each other. Even though relationship with other people has its challenges, it also has its rewards. Forgive us for losing sight of Your desire for us to live life with each other, to be different than the world—and forgive me if I've contributed to it in any way. Help me to be more like Jesus, seeking Your best for each person I meet and defending Your truth with wisdom and grace.

• • •

God, You call us as Your people to "go and be reconciled" with our fellow Christians (Matthew 5:24 NIV). We all need to be reconciled, first with You, and then, as an ongoing habit, with others. I want to be a peacemaker. You have given me authority and ability to represent You as Your son wherever I am. Help me to avoid arguments and quarreling, but also help me to remind others that negative words only cause harm and divide the church. You want unity in the essentials, liberty in non-essentials, and charity in all things.

Lord, give me the discernment to identify troublemakers and the courage to confront them—to "note those who cause divisions and offenses, contrary to the doctrine which you learned, and avoid them" (Romans 16:17 NKJV). When I can't avoid them, give me the words to remind them that You want unity in the church, and "to stop fighting over words. Such arguments are useless, and they can ruin those who hear them" (2 Timothy 2:14 NLT).

• • •

Father, I find myself tempted to give into divisive behavior at church. Forgive me for leaving gossip unquestioned or for taking offense when there is none—reading things into people's words that aren't there. I should be going directly to a person if I have an issue with him (Matthew 18)—and asking others if they've done the same. I will take the high and narrow road because that's Your path, Jesus, and I want to be more like You.

DEATH OF A CHILD

The LORD is near to the brokenhearted
and saves the crushed in spirit.
PSALM 34:18 ESV

• • •

There's no rulebook for dealing with the loss of a child. Emotions vary from silent shock to nervous breakdown—and every shade of black in between. While the intensity of the feelings over the loss lessens over time, you never get completely over it—nor should you. You never imagined this, never planned for it, and, even with God's help, rebuilding your life will still be one of the hardest things you've ever done. But in this dark hour, know this: God is suffering with you in the deepest possible way. Remember, He lost a child once too. He knows the darkness and the silence that comes, and He knows it's something no words can lift, or should even try to. He understands that you feel helpless and even abandoned, and He can take your anger and your hard questions. Let Him heal you in His time and by His Spirit, His Word, and His people.

Heavenly Father, through my child You taught me
how to love. Now, teach me how to grieve and to heal.
You give and You take away, but I will still praise Your name.

• • •

Lord God, I'm so grateful for the time You gave me with my child. In
the time we had, I was changed forever. My heart was made fuller,
my eyes were opened wider, and my faith was made stronger. I'm
overwhelmed with fond memories and gratitude, which I will carry
for the rest of my life in a way that honors my dear one and You.

• • •

God, I'm struggling to find words. I don't know what to pray, how
to pray, or, honestly, even why to pray. I can't imagine why You
let my child die. I don't know if I should ask You for strength to
endure because part of me wants to die and be with my baby
again. I don't know if I should ask You for healing because we
both know this pain will never completely heal, at least not here
on earth. Right now, it's best if I let You pray: "But if we hope for
what we do not see, we wait for it with patience. Likewise the
Spirit helps us in our weakness. For we do not know what to pray
for as we ought, but the Spirit himself intercedes for us with
groanings too deep for words" (Romans 8:25–26 ESV).

Jesus, I live in the hope of resurrection. You've promised that You are working all things together for good, and while I can't begin to imagine how my child's death fits into that, I know that when I see You, I will be reunited with my precious one.

• • •

Lord, this not a simple situation, but then You are not a simple God. Right now, all I have to offer You is my tears, none of which seem to fill the emptiness in my heart. I trust that You are grieving with me, that You are in fact "a man of sorrows, acquainted with deepest grief" (Isaiah 53:3 NLT).

• • •

Father, give me the strength I need to be there for my family. I never thought I could hurt this much, but my wife and other kids still need me. They see me hurting, but they are grieving too. They need me to be there through all the painful "firsts" of our new normal—first birthday, first Christmas, first beginning of the school year. I need to set the tone for talking about my child with them and with others, so I need Your Spirit and Your words more than ever.

DEATH OF A PARENT

All praise to the God and Father of our Master, Jesus the Messiah! Father of all mercy! God of all healing counsel! He comes alongside us when we go through hard times, and before you know it, he brings us alongside someone else who is going through hard times so that we can be there for that person just as God was there for us. We have plenty of hard times that come from following the Messiah, but no more so than the good times of his healing comfort—we get a full measure of that, too.

2 Corinthians 1:3–5 msg

• • •

Some cultural stigma still exists around men properly grieving death—as if we should just carry on like nothing of significance has happened. The unintended result is that we diminish the significance of the people we need to grieve.

In many ways, we're never quite as ready as we might think for a parent to die. Aside from any questions of mercy or timing, as a man you need to create space to pause and honor the parent who has died. Whether or not yours were good parents, whether or not they raised you well, or whether or not they were good Christian examples, God brought you to life through them. He doesn't make mistakes. To mourn the loss of a parent, then, is to honor God's greater purposes and ultimate glory—in your life, and in all the lives you affect.

Father, I am so grateful for the time I had with my parents,
for all the memories, and for everything they taught me,
especially about You. Even though I miss them terribly, the
thought of them being with You, healed and whole, blesses me
tremendously. Thank You for the hope of the resurrection,
of the reunion to come, and of peace in the face of grief.

• • •

Even as I grieve, Lord, and miss my parent terribly, I'm thankful
for him. I want to honor him, and I want his legacy of godliness to
continue in me and in my children. Help me to find the best ways
to be there for my remaining parent, to understand the power and
depth of that parent's grief, and to come alongside that parent in
meaningful ways. Comfort my remaining parent in this time of
sorrow and as he or she begins to adjust to life without a spouse.
Let it be in as healthy a way as possible.

• • •

I'm shaken, God. It's hard for me to think of myself as an orphan.
I'm so used to being independent, even to being the one who
helped my parents out. But it's hard to believe they're gone. If I'm
honest, I feel a little like a kid again, scared of the dark because
the people who taught me to face it are gone. I know You are with
me, though, and I'm glad. I need You now more than ever.

*God, I don't know if my parent was a believer. I will trust
that to You. As Abraham said, "Should not the Judge of all the
earth do what is right?" (Genesis 18:25 NLT). The thought of the
"right thing," though, is painful. It puts a knot in my stomach
and a lump in my throat. Help me to see Your justice—to see
that You are holy, that You are good, and that You don't do
anything that won't someday make sense.*

. . .

*I'm feeling guilty, Lord, thinking of missed opportunities.
I didn't do everything I could have for my parents. I didn't love
them the way I should have, didn't spend the time with them.
And now they're gone. I own that, but I can't bear the weight.
Forgive me, Father. Teach me how to live with what I can't change,
how to leave those regrets and hard feelings with You. Show
me how to make things right with the people in my life.*

DEATH OF A PET

Don't be afraid, for I am with you. Don't be discouraged,
for I am your God. I will strengthen you and help you.
I will hold you up with my victorious right hand.

Isaiah 41:10 NLT

• • •

The death of a pet can have a powerful impact. So often, we truly invest ourselves in our pets—spending time, money, and emotion to pay back a little of what they offer us in companionship, character, and affection. Even though a pet is very much a member of the family, unsympathetic people sometimes belittle the pain losing one brings.

But your loss matters to God. He created and cares for animals: "Every animal of the forest is mine, and the cattle on a thousand hills" (Psalm 50:10 NIV). Furthermore, *your* feelings matter to Him. When the loss of a beloved animal companion hurts you, it hurts Him too. And while animals don't have souls the way humans do, they are creatures of surprising emotional capacity and can have deep impact on our lives.

Our love for our pets is a little like God's love for us. That someone so far above and beyond us should embrace us for who we are is humbling and a cause for rejoicing. We're a lot like God when we love our pets well. Their loss is worth mourning because they, as God's creation, matter.

Lord God, I feel a strange push-pull at the loss of my pet.
I miss him terribly, but it's hard to share that with people who
see my grief over the loss of an animal as silly or unimportant.
But I know what my pet meant to me. And I know that You are
a giver of good gifts. Thank You for the time I had with my pet,
for all the memories and companionship. And thank You for
giving me a chance to love another living being so selflessly.
I gained so much from someone who had only love to offer.

• • •

Father, my family is grieving the loss of our beloved pet.
As each of us mourns in our own way, I want to set the right
tone—a healthy recognition of what our companion meant
to us along with a healthy process of grieving. Give me
the right words to say to my wife and kids.

God, I am devastated at the loss of my pet. It's like I can't go anywhere in the house, or even in my car, without thinking of the time we spent together. I don't know if I could miss even a human relative like this. I loved my pet without condition or reservation, and in this imperfect, broken world, I feel the loss of that as much as anything. I need Your comfort, Lord.

• • •

Lord, as I mourn the loss of my pet, I think of the lessons about unconditional love You taught me during our time together. That wonderful animal greeted me with enthusiasm, sought comfort in my presence, and enriched my life through a whole slew of memorable moments. My pet had nothing to offer me in terms of financial gain, corporate advancement, or social status, but his presence gave me joy. Maybe that's a little like how You feel about me. Thanks for loving me like that. I will try to do better about being glad to come into Your presence in prayer, worship, and reading Your Word—and I know I'll be glad to see You when that day finally comes.

DEATH OF A WIFE

He heals the brokenhearted and binds up their wounds.
PSALM 147:3 NKJV

• • •

Losing your wife creates a single wound that cuts to your core—and a thousand lesser wounds that you only become aware of as time passes and her absence pierces you again and again. The grief can feel like learning to breathe underwater, but the world continues to spin, and even though you understand that God is right there with you, it all feels wrong.

If you've got kids at home, they need you more than ever. And then there's all the paperwork and arrangements. There's not enough time in the world to grieve, but people need you. . . and you need them. Take a breath. Take another breath. God is that close to you. He knows all the things you remember and all the things you can't say. Let Him bind your wounds.

I feel like I'm always wet with grief, Father. Sometimes the water just dampens my feet, and other times it covers me. The water is high today, Lord, and I'm too weak to tread it, much less swim. Hold me up and help me to keep breathing. "Heal me, Lord, and I will be healed; save me and I will be saved, for you are the one I praise" (Jeremiah 17:14 NIV).

• • •

Jesus, You told me to love my enemies, but I am glad that death is the enemy I don't have to learn how to love. In the last day, when You return and humble all Your enemies, "the last enemy to be destroyed is death" (1 Corinthians 15:26 NLT). I rejoice now that the foe that took my wife—even if it's just for a season— will be conquered. By Your resurrection, You have taken death's sting forever, and I look forward to the day in eternity when You hold one hand and my wife holds the other.

God, I'm numb. Saying I miss my wife is a little like saying I miss breathing normally. Everything is just off. I don't know what thought scares me more—feeling nothing or feeling everything. Like the psalmist said, my flesh and my heart are failing, but You, God, are my strength (Psalm 73:26). You will give me what I need to keep going and to feel again in time.

• • •

Father, help me to honor my wife by grieving her properly. I know she wouldn't want me to shut down, but sometimes I just have to. Even though I know she's with You, happy and pain-free, I'm still here, missing my friend, my lover, my helper. Jesus said, "Blessed are those who mourn, for they will be comforted" (Matthew 5:4 NIV). I will miss her for the rest of my life, but I know You still have things for me to do in this life, and she would want me to do them. That's all fine and good, but now I just need You to comfort me.

DEPRESSION

It is the LORD who goes before you. He will be with you; he will not leave you or forsake you. Do not fear or be dismayed.

DEUTERONOMY 31:8 ESV

• • •

Many Christians tend to dismiss depression as a self-pitying attitude or the result of a lack of prayer or time spent reading the Bible. However, depression is very real. It might be temporary or ongoing, clinical or spiritual, or a potent cocktail made up of a variety of factors and circumstances accumulating in your life during a particular season.

Ironically, the Bible contains many examples of people suffering depression. Look at Elijah after his battle with the prophets of Baal, or David at various points in his life (pursued by a jealous and dangerous Saul or shamed by his adultery with Bathsheba, for example). Even the sons of Korah, whose job it was to write and perform worship songs in the temple, experienced serious low points (Psalms 42–43). All of them, however, found strength in God and in fellowship.

Don't be ashamed to seek help from a doctor or Christian counselor for your depression. And remember, God is with you always. When the waves overwhelm you or the storm surrounds you, hold fast to His hope.

I'm feeling low today, Father. The louder thoughts I'm having tell me I'm alone, that there's no way out. Turn up the volume of Your voice, Father. I'm desperate to hear from You, whether it's in Your Word or through someone else. Give me the strength the psalmist had when he wrote, "Why am I so discouraged? Why is my heart so sad? I will put my hope in God! I will praise him again— my Savior and my God!" (Psalm 42:5–6 NLT).

• • •

Lord, I am beginning to think I'm depressed. Someone concerned about me brought up the possibility, but I hadn't wanted to admit it up till now. I've been through hard times before, but I've never felt like this—like things are getting worse and won't ever get better. I'm caught in a loop of emotions—sadness, anger, frustration, even despair—and it feels like my prayers are bouncing off the ceiling. Hear me, Lord. I'm trying to believe that You are with me; help my unbelief (Mark 9:24). Give me the courage to seek help. Please put someone in my path who can help me get a grip on this.

Give me strength and peace, Lord. A lot's been going on,
and even though I'm seeking help to fight this depression,
today is just a black dog kind of day. I trust that You have Your
reasons for allowing me to suffer this way, that You can use my
hardship to comfort someone else in a similar space, and that
You will make me stronger—or at least more willing and able
to rely wholeheartedly on You. God, You are my healer,
my redeemer, my friend. I need You today.

• • •

God, I know You are with me, but I confess, I've been thinking
some about what it would be like to be with You. . .in heaven.
I know that You wouldn't want me to take my own life, but I just
want the pain to stop. I can't manage it anymore. I don't want to
die, but living hurts so much. Step in, God, and save me! "For the
grave cannot praise you, death cannot sing your praise; those who
go down to the pit cannot hope for your faithfulness" (Isaiah 38:18
NIV). I want to be among "the living, the living—they praise you, as I
am doing today; parents tell their children about your faithfulness"
(v. 19). Glorify Yourself, Lord—give me a reason to praise
You today, a reason to keep going.

DISABILITIES

We can rejoice, too, when we run into problems and trials, for we know that they help us develop endurance. And endurance develops strength of character, and character strengthens our confident hope of salvation. And this hope will not lead to disappointment. For we know how dearly God loves us, because he has given us the Holy Spirit to fill our hearts with his love.

ROMANS 5:3–5 NLT

· · ·

Even though the Bible recounts many instances of Jesus and His disciples healing various disabilities, it also includes many stories of God working in and through people marked by them. God has plans and purposes for each of His children—in every stage of life and circumstance in which they find themselves. In that sense, we can see that not every disability is necessarily negative.

God cares about each of us as we are. He alone knows into what He might make us. We are all created in God's image, and are equal in His eyes without regard to gender, age, ethnicity, socioeconomic status, or able-bodiedness. A disability, there-fore, isn't necessarily a curse or the wages of sin, but often a challenge through which God might be glorified and a vehicle to teach lessons of grace to anyone with the heart to receive them. If you or someone you know is facing complex physical and emotional challenges, remember that God is faithful to complete a work He started regardless of either physical ability or limitation.

Lord, as a disabled man in a world that values physical ruggedness and accomplishment, remind me that my value is not based on what I can do but on what You can do through me. You said You would use the things the world considers weak to trip up the things it considers strong (1 Corinthians 1:26–29). Let Your strength and wisdom mark my life, so that my disadvantage becomes an advantage in bringing You glory and in advancing Your kingdom.

• • •

Father, it's hard for me to find a place to belong. I know I'm Yours, a member of the body of Christ, but people often don't know how to approach me. I know I'm different, but I also know You don't make mistakes. You made me like this for Your good reasons, and I want to serve You. I want to love and be loved by Your people, to be missed when I'm not there, and to be supported when things go wrong—and to miss others and support them in turn. I want to be Your man in my community. Give me Your wisdom, Your heart for others, and the peace of Your Spirit as I wait on Your timing.

Jesus, thank You for touching and embracing those the world consider outcasts when You came to earth. Everyone on earth needs You, but You've allowed me a pretty stark reminder that not everyone appreciates that. Thank You for the fellowship of Your suffering. Thank You that I know what it's like to be rejected and despised just for being who I am. You came looking for me, though, to save me from sin, and You love me as I am. In the world's eyes, it's a total longshot that a guy like me could ever become much of anything. But in Your eyes, I'm worth Your very life. I want to see people who think I'm nothing through Your eyes and with Your heart, and love them with the grace You showed me.

* * *

God, You have seen fit to bring someone with a disability into my life. I don't want to shirk the responsibility I have to treat everyone I meet with respect and honor (Philippians 2:3–4), but I admit I don't really know where or how to start. Your Word tells me "to do justly, to love mercy, and to walk humbly" with You (Micah 6:8 NKJV). I want to go beyond just including people with disabilities at church, but to also do what I can to make sure they know they belong and that we are willing to learn from their experiences and wisdom. Help me to listen well, to learn more, and to fight the distinction of "them and us." We are Your children, all of us valued parts of the body of Christ.

Father, all of us deal with a disability at some point or another. Whether it's temporary or permanent, You're aware of it and Your purposes are in it. Whatever brings it on—age, trauma, congenital defect—we all have value to You in every stage of our lives, and You can bring value to everything we must endure. Such a time has come upon me. I'm having to take stock of how I saw myself before—all the things I thought made me important that I don't have or can't do now. Like Paul, I ask You for deliverance, relief, and healing—but like Paul, I want to embrace the truth that Your grace is sufficient for me (2 Corinthians 12:9).

DISAPPOINTMENT

Humble yourselves in the sight of
the Lord, and He will lift you up.
JAMES 4:10 NKJV

• • •

Disappointment is a heavy burden to bear, but it's one all Christian men know well. You pray and prepare and dare to dream and hope—and then the unexpected hits. And you think, *Why does God so often say "no" or "wait"?* Disappointments pile up and then become discouragement.

God knows you're bummed out, and He doesn't want you to keep it to yourself. Let Him know, even if only to keep the bitterness from taking hold in your heart. Wouldn't it be great if you always prayed for things that God could say "yes" to? Sure, but only the Holy Spirit can do that. But in the meantime, trust the Lord. He knows you and your future, and He will guide you when You ask Him "What's next?" instead of "Why me?"

God, I'm bringing the weight of my disappointment to You. I did the best I could do—I prayed, read the Bible, sought godly counsel— and it wasn't enough to bring the result I wanted. I have all sorts of questions, but the one I need to be asking is, "What now, Lord?" Bring me something or someone to point out the next step, whatever it may be. I trust You.

• • •

Lord, help me to understand that my disappointment is not because You've let me down but because my expectations weren't met. I don't want to get on a rollercoaster of resentment and cynicism, blame-shifting and grudge-holding my way to a bitter end. So, I'm giving You my sadness and disappointment because I don't want it to get the better of me. I don't want to stop giving my best or stop expecting the best from You or others. I trust that You are working all things together for good, taking into account all the details and issues and personalities that I could never be aware of or fully anticipate. I will expect You to be true to Yourself— and that's more than enough for me.

Father, I am struggling to let go of my disappointment. All I can think of is the opportunity missed, the circumstances that resulted, and the people who let me down. And now I'm stuck in the why of it all. That's not where You want me to be, but I don't know how to get unstuck. I need Your perspective—or at least someone wiser than I am to come alongside me and help me get out of my own head and help me regain a biblical perspective. I am disappointed, but because You are my God, I am not defeated (Romans 8:31–39).

• • •

Only You can meet all my needs, God. I'm caught between my expectations and my circumstances, and I'm not happy with either. I didn't think this is where I would be at this point in my life and I'm frustrated. I give my frustration to You, though. I want to "give thanks in all circumstances; for this is God's will for you in Christ Jesus" (1 Thessalonians 5:18 NIV). Thank You that I am Yours, that You make good things come out of bad things, that You have good plans for my future, and that You care about me right now.

DISHONESTY

"And what do you benefit if you gain the
whole world but lose your own soul?"

MARK 8:36 NLT

• • •

A lie always circles back on you. It's easy to rejoice in the justice of other people's lies coming back to bite them, but what about when yours catch up with you? The Bible makes it clear that honesty is the best, most God-pleasing policy (Proverbs 11:3, Romans 13:7, and James 5:12, for starters).

When you come face to face with your own dishonesty, you should thank God you didn't get away with it. The repercussions for your dishonesty—whether it's just the Spirit's conviction or something more serious that affects your relationships or job or others—are God's way of trying to right your ship.

At the heart of dishonesty is distrust. At some point, you decided that God wasn't really looking out for you—your advancement, your rep (even at church)—so you tilted the playing field a bit. But God hates lying because He sees the full ramifications. He sees dishonesty as a reflection of Eden's brokenness and an imitation of the father of lies, Satan. Make a clean break now. Confess your dishonesty, make the situation right if you can, and then commit yourself to God's way. Love the truth, fill your heart with it, and trust God to guard your heart as you defend it.

Lord God, I confess my dishonesty. I have never thought of myself as deceitful, but I see now that my dishonesty is a sin—first and foremost, against You. I've misrepresented You. You're a God of order, not chaos; light, not darkness; and truth, not lies. All the dishonest ways I've tried to build myself up or satisfy my desires have built walls between me and You, and between me and others. The real me isn't as attractive as the image I've created, but that image was an idol to my ego. I forsake it and choose You. Nothing is hidden from You, and yet You still love me. I want to live honestly before You. Even if it's a broken, ugly version of me, at least it will be an honest one—and that means a forgiven, redeemed man constantly in need of Your grace and love.

$$\cdot \ \cdot \ \cdot$$

Father, forgive me for my lies. I've built an image of myself that reflects the incomplete image I've formed of You—someone who winks at little white lies, who sees half-truths as a necessary evil in a broken world. I thought I was getting ahead, but I've forgotten Your holiness—and that You call me to be like You. And You've never lied and never will. I want to fill my heart with Your truth instead: "Brothers, whatever is true, whatever is honorable, whatever is just, whatever is pure, whatever is lovely, whatever is commendable, if there is any excellence, if there is anything worthy of praise, think about these things" (Philippians 4:8 ESV).

God, I've been affected by someone else's dishonesty. My reputation has suffered, and the thought of it makes me angry. I'm not saying I'm perfect, but I feel blindsided and I want to defend myself. My mind is a maze of arguments and frustrations, and I don't trust myself to represent You well right now. Will You defend me instead? Will You remember all the times and ways I've tried to stay true to You and Your Word, forgive me for the times I've failed, and uphold me for Your name's sake? I will wait on You.

• • •

Lord, help me to own my mistakes and to think about what it's like to be on the other side of me. I've tried to cover my mistakes by shifting the blame or misrepresenting what others have said or done. I haven't fooled anyone, but I have broken trust. Forgive me for drifting from Your Word and ways. I want to be honest in my dealings, but it's a day-to-day process of making lots of small decisions: managing my time and expectations, circling back on hard issues, trusting that You will bring good things when I make a habit of loving others by seeking their best welfare consistently, which You have called me to do.

DISTRUST

*It is better to trust in the L*ORD
than to put confidence in man.
PSALM 118:8 NKJV

• • •

At times, we all fall short of trustworthiness. We trust our-selves—our own thoughts and understanding—rather than God. We trust our feelings over God's truth and lies over the difficulty of living by that truth. We trust wealth and power and self-sufficiency instead of God's provision.

All those things—ourselves, people, and things—will let us down at some point. But God never will. And even though trust is crucial to healthy human relationships, the Bible doesn't tell us to fully trust anyone other than God (with the notable exception of the trust shared between husbands and wives)—rather, it tells us to *love* others. Trust and promises go together, not trust and love. Only God keeps all His promises, so only He deserves our total trust. By contrast, we can love people without being able to trust them.

Part of rebuilding trust is being trustworthy. Love in a way that shows you can be trusted—even to the extent that others are convicted of their lack of reliability. When people prove themselves untrustworthy, the question isn't whether you will ever trust them again as much as will you continue to *love* them—to seek their highest good. After all, that's what God does with you.

Lord, I acknowledge that I have the universal human tendency to trust myself rather than You, to rely on my own abilities and good intentions instead of Your sovereign goodness and care. As a result, I have broken promises and proven myself untrustworthy. My ego is bruised, but the truth that only You are completely trustworthy has pricked my conscience. You have called me to reflect Your love and Your desire for forgiveness and restoration, so help me to make things right with the people I've hurt.

● ● ●

Father, I am struggling to trust my wife. There have been past hurts, and I feel myself withdrawing from her. I feel like I have to be careful around her, that I can't rely on her to do what she says she will do. I often feel myself being critical of her, which is usually a sign that I need to check my own heart. Show me if I am being untrustworthy in any way—if I am not making her feel safe or cared for. Successful marriages are built on trust. Your Word says of a godly wife that the "heart of her husband trusts in her, and he will have no lack of gain" (Proverbs 31:11 ESV). We need honesty between us, even if it's painful at first, and accountability so we can move forward together.

God, someone close to me has broken trust with me. It's painful to realize that this person isn't who I thought he was. I forgive him, but I ask for Your wisdom in dealing with him in the future. I also need to ask Your forgiveness, for I trusted this person's promises because they sounded good, and I didn't trust You enough to ask what You thought about them. I want to be more like You—able to love when I and others prove untrustworthy.

* * *

Lord, I am dealing with the fallout of broken trust. What someone has done constantly swirls around in my mind, and I'm struggling to control my hurt and anger. Your Word reminds me to trust in You with all of my heart and not to lean on my own limited understanding, but I need You to get me back on course (Proverbs 3:4–6). I need to let go and forgive this person. I don't want to become an untrusting person, but I need Your discernment so I can know whether or not to give the benefit of the doubt. Even if this person never regains my trust, I need to show him or her the mercy and grace You've so often shown me.

* * *

God, as I think about the difficult situation I'm in, and the disappointment and frustration I feel, I realize that this isn't Your fault but mine. As much as it hurts to say so, I haven't trusted You, even though You have saved me from sin and provided for me so many times and in so many ways. I tried to do this in my own strength and came up short. Forgive me. I will seek Your will in Your Word and in godly counsel. And, yes, I will ask You what You want me to do before I undertake my next challenge.

DIVORCE/SEPARATION

"I hate divorce," says the God of Israel. God-of-the-Angel-Armies says, "I hate the violent dismembering of the 'one flesh' of marriage." So watch yourselves. Don't let your guard down. Don't cheat.

MALACHI 2:16 MSG

· · ·

The prospect of divorce is terribly difficult, complicated, and painful. It clearly qualifies as a major trial of life, and in that sense, a Christian should approach it as he would any other hardship: by seeking God in prayer and His Word, by seeking godly advice from pastors or professional counselors, and by remembering that God's heart always points toward reconciliation and restoration.

The emotional and spiritual battles around a broken marriage are even more intense than other life crises, simply because God's design for marriage is that it should reflect the relationship between Jesus and His church—something Satan would dearly love to destroy. In some cases, sin might make separation necessary, but move warily, carefully, and prayerfully. If you are willing to trust God with this incredibly difficult situation, He will help you do the right thing—not the easy thing, but the right thing. So wait on Him, pray fervently for His will, get help from your pastor or counselor, and work toward removing any obstacles to reconciliation and restoration. Guard your spirit and stay true to your marriage vows. Then, trust God to protect and restore what He loves—you, your wife, and your marriage.

Lord, divorce is not the unpardonable sin, but it's not what You want for me either. I admit that there are times when divorce seems like the only way to deal with my relationship with my wife. I know the current state of my marriage didn't develop overnight, and I know it won't be resolved right away either. Regardless of the cause, and regardless of whether there is biblical support for ending my marriage, I commit myself to seeking Your will for my marriage.

• • •

God, I have not always walked in Your ways, and that is partly why my marriage is falling apart. I have no peace and no joy at the thought of getting separated or divorced, but I don't know how to fix my marriage either. You want me to walk according to Your ways, to seek Your counsel in Your Word and through godly ministers and counselors. You want me to be wise and patient and to put my wife's needs ahead of my own—all things I confess that I haven't done consistently in our marriage. These are desperate times for us, Father, so help me be the man You want me to be and the husband my wife needs me to be (even if she won't recognize me playing that role). Save my marriage.

Father, when my parents got divorced, I promised myself I would never let that happen in my own marriage. But here I am, in danger of wounding my own kids in the very same ways my parents wounded me when they divorced. I still love my parents, and I know my kids would still love me if my wife and I divorced, but I am desperate to avoid the emotional and spiritual tsunami breaking up my family unit would cause. I need to remember that Your love lasts, that You keep Your commitments and expect me to keep mine, and that You can make a way where there seems no way. I want to break this cycle of divorce in my family history, but I can't do it without You.

• • •

Jesus, I need to take an unflinching look at how my behavior is damaging my marriage. You said that my wife and I "are no longer two but one flesh. Therefore what God has joined together, let not man separate" (Matthew 19:6 NKJV). I have said things, looked at things, and done things that threaten to shatter a bond You meant to be permanent in this life. If You responded to me based on the way I've responded to my wife, You would have revoked my salvation by now. I'm so grateful You never will, and I want for my marriage the forgiveness and reconciliation You offered me.

• • •

Holy Spirit, show me the truth about myself and give me the courage not to flinch. I will own my sin, confess it, and turn from it, getting any help I need to do so. I want to show my wife evidence of change, and I want to avoid separation or divorce. It'll take time, so help her to be as patient and gracious with me as You have been. Fill me, lead me, and give me the words to rebuild what's been damaged.

DOUBT

But when you ask, you must believe and not doubt,
because the one who doubts is like a wave of the sea,
blown and tossed by the wind.

<small>JAMES 1:6 NIV</small>

• • •

Doubt is a reality for all people—even Christians. We're just among the least likely to admit it. That's because some folks confuse doubt for dissent or disbelief—and while doubt can lead to both, it isn't either, in and of itself. There's a big difference between doubt that comes from wondering how to live out your faith and doubt that questions the doctrinal truths of your faith. In fact, the right kind of doubt (the first kind) can lead to truth.

Some of history's most effective believers started as doubters, from the apostle Thomas to Augustine of Hippo to C.S. Lewis, Lee Strobel, and Philip Yancey. When you bring your honest doubt before God, He can use it to develop dependency on Him, turning your turmoil to trust. That's a good description of faith. The writer of Hebrews wrote, "Without faith *it is* impossible to please *Him*, for he who comes to God must believe that He is, and *that* He is a rewarder of those who diligently seek Him" (Hebrews 11:6 NKJV). Start with what you know is true about God and go from there.

Lord, I am relieved that doubt and faith are not incompatible.
But I'm having a hard time seeing You at work lately. I admit
I've been disappointed in the way some things have worked out—
things I prayed and searched Your Word about—but I sympathize
with the dad in the Bible who prayed, "Lord, I believe;
help my unbelief!" (Mark 9:24 NKJV).

• • •

Father, I am beginning to understand that faith is not a matter of
certainty but belief. I don't need to know everything about Your
decision-making process or the factors You take into account (I
doubt my mind could handle the scope of all that!). I've had doubts
about some things I've heard Christians say, and questions about
things I've read in Your Word. I confess that I've settled for people's
interpretations of Your character and the Bible instead of seeking
answers from You myself. I trust that You are good, sovereign, holy,
loving, merciful, just, righteous, and gracious, and that if I search
for You with all my heart, I'll find You (Jeremiah 29:13).

God, I'm looking at the world around me and I see that it's a mess. Politics, war, terrorism, cultural issues, poverty, racism— it's all overwhelming to me. I've tried to learn about the issues and what Christians should do about them, and I've even tried to get involved and make a difference, but the problems remain. If anything, they feel even bigger and more oppressive. I give You my fear and guilt and frustration—and my doubt that I can make any kind of impact for You. I'm not sure what else to do, except ask You to walk with me. Walk with me, Lord.

• • •

God, I'm praying not because I'm convinced it makes the difference Your Word says it does but because I'm more anxious that if I don't, my faith will fail. I talk to You and wait for an answer, but I can't tell whether or not You've responded. I'll accept any answer You give me; I just want to hear one. When I try to be quiet, nothing happens, and my doubting thoughts creep back in. I believe You can do anything, but I'm worried You won't. I don't want to tell anyone else my doubts because I'm afraid they'll confirm my fears—that I've lost my faith. I think I've crossed that line James warned about—the one about being double-minded (James 1:8)— which might be why I feel so unstable. Forgive me for that kind of doubt, but I'm slipping and I need You to help me forsake my unbelief. Strengthen my faith.

DRUG ABUSE

*"Because of God's tender mercy, the morning light
from heaven is about to break upon us, to give light
to those who sit in darkness and in the shadow of
death, and to guide us to the path of peace."*

Luke 1:78–79 nlt

. . .

Jesus came to set you free, to rescue you from your sin and
reconcile you with your heavenly Father. To receive Him as Lord
and Savior is to be delivered from sin and hell immediately.
But sometimes, deliverance from old habits and addictions
is a lengthier process. God might break the shackles of your
drug addiction the first time you ask Him, or He might allow
it to take longer. Your salvation isn't in question, but your fight
will be part of your journey with Him.

Through all the ups and downs, He will never leave you
or give up on you, so don't give up on Him. Eliminate all the
things that tether you to your addiction, whether it's dangerous
relationships or oppressive remnants from the past—movies,
music, books. . .anything that turns your thoughts from God.
Replace these things with God-centered relationships and
support and inspiring music and books. This is the fight of
your life—and Christ's blood proves you are worth the effort.

Jesus, You make all things new, including me. Thank You for Your Spirit in me, guiding me, teaching me Your truth, and stepping up for me in prayer (Romans 8:26–27). I see my drug abuse for the rebellion against You that it is. I see now that I chose darkness instead of Your light for too long. I need Your light now to push the drugs out of my system, and I need You to give me the desire to take them out of my mind. I am a new and good man in You, Jesus.

• • •

Lord God, I am humbled that You lowered Yourself to my level to show me how much You love me. You have been with me in some very dark places and times, and I owe You everything. I trust the timing of Your deliverance from my addiction to drugs. Cleanse me from any need for them and any desire to take them. Protect me from my worst impulses and the physical ache of my dependency. You are my strength and my shelter.

Father, I know You want me to be healthy and whole. But I also know that the devil is after me, like a lion on the prowl (1 Peter 5:8–11). I commit to standing firm against my addiction, to being on the alert for warning signs, and to giving You all my worries and troubles. Set my feet on Your firm foundation.

* * *

God, set me free from the fear and anger that drove me to a life of drug addiction. I have been consumed with a burning need for drugs at different times, and I've made compromises, excuses, and mistakes that have hurt me and others and that have separated me from my family, friends, and You. Deliver me from the false acceptance of my addiction as insurmountable. Nothing is impossible for You (Matthew 19:26). I need You, God, and You alone can save me. Forgive me, heal me, and lead me to the help and support I need to fight my addiction.

DYSFUNCTIONAL RELATIONSHIPS

Go out into the world uncorrupted, a breath of fresh air
in this squalid and polluted society. Provide people
with a glimpse of good living and of the living God.

PHILIPPIANS 2:15 MSG

• • •

Some relationships just seem destined to go off the rails. One person's negative, immature behavior derails the healthy functioning of a family or a relationship at work or church. Dysfunction begets more dysfunction; hurt people hurt other people.

Unconsciously, we re-create the unhealthy drama we grew up with, picking up relationships with other dysfunctional people because we're not even aware there's a better way. But there is: God's way.

As a Spirit-filled believer, you have more discernment than you think—so stop ignoring it. Discover the core of your fears—self-esteem, intimacy, abandonment, being alone, commitment—and get help to address it. Remember, God's love lives in you: "There is no fear in love, but perfect love casts out fear. For fear has to do with punishment, and whoever fears has not been perfected in love" (1 John 4:18 ESV). God's perfect love will help you break sin's dysfunction and create healthy, functional relationships.

Lord, You know I grew up in a very messed-up family. There was no emotional or spiritual balance, starting with my parents. We were a case study for Proverbs 11:29 (msg): "Exploit or abuse your family, and end up with a fistful of air; common sense tells you it's a stupid way to live." I'm starting to see some of the same patterns in my own family, though I swore it would be different. I want it to be different. Help me identify where the problems are, and then help me take steps to create a mature, responsible, healthy set of relationships. Bring me people who can teach me differently and hold me accountable.

• • •

God, one of Your most important instructions to us fathers is not to "exasperate" our children, but I'm falling short of that. When my kids are disrespectful, I respond with anger and harsh words. I know my anger doesn't accomplish Your purposes in any of our lives (James 1:20). Forgive me, help me to forgive my children, and let their hearts be forgiving toward me. I need to focus on bringing them up "in the discipline and instruction of the Lord" (Ephesians 6:4 esv). I know that kind of discipline begins with me showing self-control and wisdom that comes from knowing You better.

• • •

God, I am struggling to change painful, repeated, dysfunctional behavior in my family. Help me see what I need to see—the patterns that need to change, both in me and in others. Guide me in taking steps toward healing and consistently healthy behavior for all of us, and lead me in finding resources and people who can advise me and hold me accountable. I am reminded that Your "divine power has given us everything we need for a godly life" (2 Peter 1:3 niv).

Father, the dynamic in my family seems out of control. I feel powerless to change the lack of harmony between me and my wife, the foolishness my kids seem committed to, and the difficulties of getting along with other family members. When I look at the Bible (even in the beginning, in Genesis), crazy, messed-up families seem more common than ones that get along and serve You well. But then I think of Your purposes in all of that. Sin has cut us off from You and led to relationships driven by selfishness. We need a Savior. Fortunately, in Jesus Christ, You gave us what we needed most and deserved least—grace, forgiveness, and hope. Let me lead my family in an ongoing experience of the grace and love that starts with You.

• • •

Lord, I need Your help getting away from a toxic relationship. Somehow, I ended up partnering with someone who is consistently negative, unethical, and generally miserable. Should I confront the behavior or just get out? I have tried to be an example of encouragement, preparation, and integrity, but to no avail. I feel like I'm endorsing this person's attitudes and actions just by being in the same room. Please show me if there is something I have done to contribute to the behavior, so I can try to make it right. Otherwise, give me the courage to speak up, and even to get out, before this person's problems poison my thinking and behavior.

ELDERLY PARENTS

*"Listen to me, O house of Jacob, all the remnant of the
house of Israel, who have been borne by me from before
your birth, carried from the womb; even to your old age
I am he, and to gray hairs I will carry you. I have made,
and I will bear; I will carry and will save."*

ISAIAH 46:3–4 ESV

• • •

Old age isn't for wimps. It's hard watching your parents deal
with all the trials and challenges that come with aging, and
even harder realizing that the people who raised you are going
to need you more than they ever have.

Because most people are now living longer, healthier
lives, chances are good you'll become involved in caring for
your parents in their old age. But while there's nothing easy
about it, there are also blessings that come with it, not the
least of which is a chance on both sides to open your hearts to
each other in new ways. God wants you to honor and love your
parents in this final stage of their lives, but He will also bless
you through them, if you are open to accepting the challenges.

Father, as my parents get older, I need to be more deliberate about spending time with them. I don't want to be one of those sons who gets so busy that he neglects the people who brought him into the world. Life is so busy, but I know I must make time for what matters most to me.

* * *

Lord, Your Word makes it clear that I owe my parents a portion of my love, time, and care as they grow older. The Bible says, "Listen to your father, who gave you life, and don't despise your mother when she is old" (Proverbs 23:22 NLT). They know what it is to be in my stage of life—busy with work and kids and activities—and, if You're willing, one day I'll know what it is to be at their stage. I commit myself to treating them with the respect and consideration I will want from my own children in my latter years. It's a privilege to care for them, and I want to do it well.

God, my parents are in a season of life where it's easy for them to become isolated. Bless them with good relationships and enjoyable social connections. Give them good health— sound minds and bodies, despite the rigors of age. Keep them connected to You, and help them to finish strong in walking with You and advancing Your kingdom.

. . .

God, it's hard to think of my parents getting older, growing frail, and getting sick. I'm not sure I'm ready for this transition to caring for them the way they cared for me as a kid. Prepare me for the coming changes. Guide me in having these hard conversations with them about what to do in a crisis, and help me to listen well and figure out how to help. This is a normal part of life, but I need Your strength to deal with it in a healthy way.

ENEMIES

"For I will give you a mouth and wisdom which all your adversaries will not be able to contradict or resist."

LUKE 21:15 NKJV

• • •

Most guys don't think of themselves as having enemies—maybe soldiers or police officers do, but for most of us, it's easy to look past what Jesus said when He told us to love our enemies (Matthew 5:43–48). But look at the context in which Jesus said that. Matthew 5 launched the Sermon on the Mount—a Christian manifesto if there ever was one. Accordingly, Jesus told us to dig beneath the surface of things—the appearance of our relationships and behaviors—and check the condition of our hearts. That includes a new standard for love, one that isn't defined by warm feelings but by a determined choice to look out for another's best interests. That's what it means for the Christian to love his enemies.

Who has annoyed or disappointed or even betrayed you? If you aren't loving that person, you've made him your enemy. Catch-22: Now you're called to seek that person's best welfare—not because he or she deserves it but because Jesus, who loved an undeserving world enough to die for it, calls you to a higher way of living.

Lord, I realize I've been harboring grudges in my heart—
making enemies simply by failing to love people the way
You've called me to. I can think of people who are not loving
me—not looking out for my best interests or being only for
themselves—but this is where the rubber meets the road,
isn't it? This is where I can stump the world and show the
difference You make in my life. But I can't do it without You.
Forgive me for my hardheartedness and give me Your heart, Lord.

• • •

Jesus, my real enemies are the flesh, the world, and the devil—
and You have overcome all of them (1 John 4:4). Everyone
needs You, and even though some deliberately set themselves
against You, I can stand against their words and behavior and still
show them a better way. I can still pray for their salvation,
still obey You when You tell me, "Do not be overcome by evil,
but overcome evil with good" (Romans 12:21 NKJV).

• • •

God, You alone know all things—including the true intentions
and thoughts of every person. I don't know why this person
treated me the way he did; I only know the effects. It hurts and
angers me, but I am in no position to judge. So, if it's possible,
I want to understand this person better. Even though I don't
like him, I know You sent Jesus to die for him. This person
matters to You, and so, he matters to me.

I'm struggling to love my enemies, God. The emotions their behavior stirs up in me are powerful—desires to pay them back in kind, fighting fire with fire, placing blame. But while they have been overwhelmed by their emotions, I will not be overcome by mine. If I treat them the way they've treated me, evil wins. I'd be sinking to their level instead of rising to Yours. It's taking all I have not to hit below the belt in my words and actions, but I need Your Spirit to help me go lower—in humility and love and grace. Let Your love in me produce repentance in them.

● ● ●

Father, You've told me not to avenge myself—that You will repay those who have wronged me (Romans 12:19). But You've also told me to go beyond that, not just to avoid seeking revenge but to feed a hungry enemy or give a thirsty one a drink, "for by so doing you will heap burning coals on his head" (v. 20 ESV). I admit that the image tickles my vengeful thoughts—forgive me, please—but I realize that You're not talking about returning an injury but snuffing out whatever impulses drove their behavior. By being kind instead of mean, I can kindle the possibility of forgiveness and reconciliation. Sounds hard, but nothing is too hard for You.

FACING DEATH

*"You don't have to wait for the End. I am, right now,
Resurrection and Life. The one who believes in me, even
though he or she dies, will live. And everyone who lives believing
in me does not ultimately die at all. Do you believe this?"*
JOHN 11:25–26 MSG

• • •

Death is inevitable, barring the return of Jesus Christ before
you die. But even Christians, knowing that death is not the
end, often fail to prepare for its impact on themselves or on
the people they will leave behind.

We should face death differently than people who don't
know the hope of the resurrection (1 Thessalonians 4:13). Even
though thinking about your own death when you're healthy
and things are going well feels like staring at the sun, you
still have to face its reality. God is in control of your life, and
talking about your death won't hasten your demise. In fact,
planning for your funeral, burial or cremation, and financial
and material transitions is one of the most loving things you
can do for your family. Let God's promises anchor you as you
face death, and let your goodbyes be your final testimony of
His goodness and bright hope.

Lord, the journey to the end is hard. I thought I would read the Bible more, pray more, minister more—really make whatever time I had left a final tour de force for Your glory. Instead, I find myself weakened, unable to concentrate long enough to read more than a few verses or utter a few words. Even though I am on the way to becoming so much more than I ever was, I feel like I am so much less. My hope is that my reliance on You for everything is reaching its fullness—that You will somehow shine that much brighter in my growing weakness (2 Corinthians 12:9).

* * *

Father, my hope is that all the practice You've given me in dying to myself will help me in the transition to eternity with You. I can't wait to see You, but the thought of going through death's door is still daunting. I know my fear of the unknown is a remnant of this sin-broken body, but I want to maintain the right balance of loss and hope in the time I have left. My gain will mean loss for my loved ones, and I ask You to comfort them and give them Your peace, now and then. Give us all Your peace.

* * *

Jesus, I'm thinking about Paul's words, "To live is Christ, and to die is gain" (Philippians 1:21 NKJV). I won't embrace death because You can still use my life as a witness to make Your name greater. Still, I am grieving now, if only because my absence will make my loved ones sad. And yet, I admit that I look forward to seeing You and hearing You assess my life, hoping You will say, "Well done, my good and faithful servant" (Matthew 25:23 NLT).

God, there's no formula for facing my death, but let me find strength in Your Word: "None of us lives to himself, and none of us dies to himself. For if we live, we live to the Lord, and if we die, we die to the Lord" (Romans 14:7–8 ESV). Come what may, I am Yours, Father.

• • •

Death brings change, Lord. There's no way around it. I've been affected by others' deaths, so it's not pride that makes me say that my death will affect other people. Their new normal will be harder than mine, though. I'll be with You—no more pain or sorrow—but they'll still be here, missing me and waiting for You. I confess, it makes me sad. All I can do is love them while I am here and trust them to Your good care.

• • •

I'm looking to Job's words for comfort today, Father: "Set a date when you'll see me again. If we humans die, will we live again? That's my question. All through these difficult days I keep hoping, waiting for the final change—for resurrection! Homesick with longing for the creature you made, you'll call—and I'll answer! You'll watch over every step I take, but you won't keep track of my missteps. My sins will be stuffed in a sack and thrown into the sea—sunk in deep ocean" (Job 14:13–17 MSG). We'll be together, and You'll give me a new, perfect version of my body, just as You did with Jesus (1 Corinthians 15). This one's getting pretty busted and worn out, so thank You, Father.

FAILURE

"Be strong and of good courage, do not fear nor be afraid of them; for the LORD your God, He is the One who goes with you. He will not leave you nor forsake you."

DEUTERONOMY 31:6 NKJV

• • •

As men, our greatest fears typically orbit around our failures—the kind that result from coming up short at school or work or in ministry. We think we've covered the bases with prayer, reading God's Word, seeking godly advice, and applying everything we have learned from experience—and sometimes, it's still not enough to accomplish our goals. It can be incredibly discouraging.

At the end of the day, though, all failure involves sin—either directly or through its general effects in the world. When David asked God to show him any hidden faults (Psalm 19), what he meant was that he could confess his sins all day long and there would still be some he had no idea existed. That's why the gospel matters so much: Christ purchased forgiveness for all our sin. Other failures happen because we come up short or face too strong an opposition, but God's grace is more than enough for us in those times too (2 Corinthians 12:7–10). God uses failure to invite us to trust Him with our hopes and dreams, and to remind us that His love for us doesn't depend on our success rate.

God, I confess that it's my ego that gets bruised when I fail. It's a reminder that I'm still striving for self-sufficiency, for some sort of merit apart from my value to You. Forgive me. Any real success I have in this world comes when I help spread the Good News of Christ, expand Your kingdom, or glorify You in my weakness. At least when I've failed there, I was shooting for a kingdom-focused goal. Let my real accomplishments be measured in relationships, beginning with my relationship with You.

• • •

Lord, my failures devastate me. I confess that I wonder where You are and why You let this happen. I fear that I am outside Your will, and I'm struggling to get my bearings and find direction. I'm trying to remember that You are good, that You work all things together for good for those who love You. It's hard for me to think that Your will for my life could include failure—that there are things I could never learn from You through success. But here we are. I will trust You, Lord, even in this. Teach me.

Father, help me figure out what kind of failure this is—a moral, spiritual failure on my part, or a defeat that has nothing to do with my walk with You. I'm not feeling particularly brave or ambitious at this point, but I am willing to deal with whatever You show me. If it's sin, I will confess it and turn from it. If it's something You're allowing me to face, I will try my best to learn what You're trying to teach me—and to remember that my priority in life is to know You better. You decide the measure of my success, not me.

. . .

God, I am trying to learn from my failure. What are You trying to develop in me? What character trait or spiritual gift or story are You building in me to use to connect with someone later? I want to be like Joshua and Caleb when they went with ten other guys to spy out Canaan. The ten all saw the giants living in the land, but only Joshua and Caleb said, "Let us go up at once and take possession, for we are well able to overcome it" (Numbers 13:30 NKJV). My only true failure would be in giving up. I will hope in You as I try again.

FAMILY FEUDS

Lead a life worthy of your calling, for you have been called by God. Always be humble and gentle. Be patient with each other, making allowance for each other's faults because of your love.

Ephesians 4:1–2 NLT

• • •

Your wife's Uncle Bob casts a shadow over Christmas and is a real turkey at Thanksgiving. He drinks too much, talks too loudly, and thinks you're a real goody two-shoes. He's driving you and everyone else nuts, and it would be easy to write him off as an impossible hard case and just put up with him—preferably as little as possible. But is there another way to deal with Bob?

Look at yourself first. Is there anything you could do differently? He may drive you crazy, but is it showing in the way you treat him? Your relatives and in-laws aren't going anywhere, so you can stew about it and dread each meeting, or you can try to make something better happen. Try a non-holiday lunch on neutral territory, or find something Bob likes to do that you can stand doing with him. Try to get to know him the way you would anyone else, asking about his job and interests. Remember, you're not perfect either. If he asks, be honest about your own challenges. Trust God to make a difference for both of you. You and Uncle Bob might never become bosom buddies, but you might be surprised to find you don't hate running into each other anymore.

God, I confess that I'm guilty of judging my problem relative. I've taken the differences in our beliefs and lifestyles and somewhere in my heart decided that I'm a better person. Like Paul wrote, "Why do you pass judgment on your brother? Or you, why do you despise your brother? For we will all stand before the judgment seat of God" (Romans 14:10 ESV). You've forgiven me, and I know I need to be more forgiving, even if my relative doesn't think he needs to be forgiven, so that I don't become bitter in my words and actions.

* * *

Father, there's a person in our family whose attitudes and behavior constantly causes conflict. I want to do something about it, but I want to do it the right way. I want to be a peacemaker, and I want to have Your heart of forgiveness and reconciliation and Your desire to pursue truth and purity. I don't want to address someone else's speck if I have a log in my eye (Matthew 7:5). Let me see myself clearly, and then guide me in approaching this person with a clean heart.

Jesus, I'm trying to practice Your attitude as I seek the best interests of someone in my family who makes my life hard (Philippians 2:4–5). I'm hoping that doing so will help me see the obstacles this person presents as opportunities to show Your love and the difference grace makes.

. . .

Lord, help me to do my best to represent You in my interactions with my own "Uncle Bob." I need Your wisdom to understand when to step up and say something and when not to, when to show grace, and when to step back from the relationship. I want to look past the frustration and disappointment I feel and approach "Bob" with kindness and humility (Galatians 6:1).

FEAR

For God has not given us a spirit of fear,
but of power and of love and of a sound mind.
2 Timothy 1:7 NKJV

• • •

The great American preacher Jonathan Edwards wrote of the balance between love and fear, "These two opposite principles of love and fear should rise and fall like the two opposite scales of a balance; when one rises the other sinks."

We face fear by trusting God, by praying instead of pacing, posturing, complaining, or compromising (1 Peter 5:7). We face fear by resting in God's goodness and timing, rather than freaking out and acting rashly. We face fear by bringing our problems to God when they arise, not after we've exhausted our energy and resources on them: "So let us come boldly to the throne of our gracious God. There we will receive his mercy, and we will find grace to help us when we need it most" (Hebrews 4:16 NLT).

Lord God, You are my shield and my strength. You are my light in the darkness, my shelter in the storm, my strength when I am weak. You shore up my mind against any enemy, whether inside my own head or outside in the world. I am a partaker of Your divine nature and promises (2 Peter 1:4). Your Word tells me not to be anxious (Philippians 4:5), and I am determined to obey You.

• • •

Jesus, I will draw You closer than my fears so I can see You instead of them. So many of the things I worry about will never happen, so I resolve to deal only with what's on my plate today. I will also get out of my own head and turn my thoughts toward serving others. I will let go of what I cannot control and trust You to protect me and my loved ones. Turn my thoughts to You.

God, I want to walk with You, hand in hand, as I face my fears.
Show me what it is that really scares me. I will give it to You and
trust You to lead, protect, and preserve me every step we take.
This is Your promise to me: "Don't be afraid, I've redeemed
you. I've called your name. You're mine. When you're in over your
head, I'll be there with you. When you're in rough waters, you will
not go down. When you're between a rock and a hard place, it
won't be a dead end—because I am God, your personal God,
the Holy of Israel, your Savior" (Isaiah 43:1–3 MSG).

* * *

Father, You are the God of second chances. I am embarrassed
at how I've let my fear get the best of me. I've let thoughts of
what could go wrong take me captive instead of taking them
captive in obedience to Christ (2 Corinthians 10:3–5). I don't
want to miss out on any experience You have for me, including
developing a deeper trust in Your protection and provision.
Give me another chance to trust You more than my fears.

FINANCIAL STRAIN

"But seek first his kingdom and his righteousness,
and all these things will be given to you as well."
MATTHEW 6:33 NIV

· · ·

While it's a good idea to listen to advice from Christian financial experts, it's an even better idea to listen to God. The Bible contains more than 2,300 verses on finances and money—so money matters to God! Open your checkbook to Him, so to speak, and let the Holy Spirit show you what needs your attention, both in your spending habits and in your attitudes about money.

The financial issues that stump you are not mysterious to God, so let Him show you His solutions. As you distinguish between your wants and needs, you'll also begin to see His divine connections come into play, and then people and resources will meet your requirements.

Financial hardship is not a time when you typically experience contentment with God's provision. It's hard wondering how or when the bills will get paid, when a new job will come along, or if serious adjustments to your lifestyle will be required. But God is aware of all of it. Honor Him first—even if your tithe shrinks along with your resources—and trust His good plans for your life.

Father, I feel the weight of money problems on my shoulders. You have given me the responsibility of providing for my family, but it seems I can't put a foot right these days. I don't want my heart to tighten up just because my wallet is shrinking. You're bigger than my bank account or my job situation or the unexpected hits our savings have taken lately. Give me Your peace as I set a tone of confidence in Your provision.

● ● ●

God, times are pretty lean these days and the bills won't stop coming. But my first debt is to You, for who You are and all You've done for me. I won't stop paying my tithe, even if we get down to the proverbial widow's mite. Like David said, "I have been young, and now am old; yet I have not seen the righteous forsaken, nor his descendants begging bread" (Psalm 37:25 NKJV).

● ● ●

Lord, I need to keep the lines of communication with my wife open about our finances. It's a sore spot and a source of conflict between us. More than ever, we need to be one flesh when it comes to money. We need to be united in searching Your Word for Your will in making decisions, in identifying problems, and in seeking solutions. Don't let money divide us, but let it draw us closer to You and each other in new and powerful ways.

God, I confess that I am hesitant to share my financial situation with anyone. I think it's because I'm also anxious about being honest with You about it. I know You're fully aware of my attitudes about money, but I ask You to show them to me. Make me aware of what I need to know and what I need to do better. I won't blink. I acknowledge that no amount of money can give me peace if I am not right with You. Forgive me for making money an idol, for letting its importance, even in the form of stress about it, take first place in my heart over You. You are my shelter and my provider. I trust You to take care of me and my family, and I will listen to any wisdom You send me.

• • •

Lord God, I've learned some hard lessons about money. One of them is that I am a steward—a caretaker—of what You've given me. You expect me to oversee what You have provided, and if I'm faithful with a little, You're faithful to give me more (Luke 16:10). Starting now, I commit myself to being responsible with my resources—my time, talent, and treasure—and to focusing on what I and my family need, rather than what we want.

FORECLOSURE

"The thief comes only to steal and kill and destroy;
I have come that they may have life, and have it to the full."
JOHN 10:10 NIV

• • •

Even if we have our eyes set on heaven, having a home is an important part of making do in this life. We want a place to lay our heads, raise our children, entertain guests, and we want it shaped to fit our personalities and tastes. There's nothing inherently wrong with any of those things—unless they become more important to us than following God's will and plan for our lives.

When you face foreclosure, some circumstances are beyond your control. Others require that you learn hard lessons about how you view and use money. Either way, it's a hard, discouraging time. Through it all, though, remember that you are a citizen of another world (Philippians 3:20), an eternal home that you're traveling toward, and no home on this earth, no matter how pleasant or rich in memories, can be more than a foretaste of what Jesus is preparing for you (John 14:1–3).

Even so, Jesus had no place to call home once His ministry began, and He knows what it's like to live without a home (Luke 9:58), to yearn for that perfect place of welcome and belonging.

Keep your eyes on Him and trust Him to provide a place for you and your family. Wherever you are, you're His family, and He is with you in this hardship.

God, we are facing foreclosure unless You intervene. It hurts to think that You led us to this home and now we're falling short. So many things beyond my control have happened, but Your Word says that my weakness is where You are strongest (2 Corinthians 12:9). Strengthen my faith through this mess. I can't get out of it without You, but I can survive whatever happens with You. I commit my home to You and trust that whatever You allow to happen, You're working it all together for my good.

* * *

Father, I have asked You over and over for help in keeping my house. Now that the foreclosure papers have come, I'm not sure how to feel. I'm disappointed, and the thought of being homeless is more than I can bear. But part of me is relieved to be out from under this debt. And still another part wants to make sure I learn whatever it is You're teaching me through this. Please help me take care of my family as we dig out from under this and find a new place to live.

Lord, I need Your strength and wisdom to lead my family at this difficult time. You came to give us life—full, overflowing life—and I don't want that to be tied to a house or a job or a savings account. You've got a bigger picture in mind than I can see. I want to lead my family in trusting You, showing Your comfort and care, and living with the faith that You will take care of us here—and that we will dwell in Your house forever (Psalm 23:6).

• • •

God, help me to be supportive and comforting to people who have gone through foreclosure. It's easy to sit off to the side and make judgments, but let me enter their suffering with them. Give me the right words to say (or the wisdom to say nothing at all). If possible, let me guide them to You, to the sure knowledge that You care, that You are listening, and that You are even more concerned about any injustice and oppression in their situation than they are. Let me be Your hands and feet to show them that You have not forgotten them.

GAMBLING

Keep your lives free from the love of money and
be content with what you have, because God has
said, "Never will I leave you; never will I forsake you."
HEBREWS 13:5 NIV

• • •

Christians are as susceptible to gambling addictions as they are to any other addiction. With gambling, what starts out as a fun diversion can quickly become a problematic dependency, even for believers. Any time we use something other than prayer and fellowship and seeking God in His Word to relieve stress, anxiety, sorrow, loneliness, or guilt, we're open to sinful addictions.

Many people enjoy the high stakes and excitement of gambling, but some are more susceptible to addiction than others. If you've ever had a problem with drinking or drugs or porn, then gambling is not a safe option for entertainment or stress relief.

Like any addiction, gambling often leads to conflict with wives and children, problems at work, and issues at church—all of which compound the guilt the gambler already feels, which can drive him further into isolation and away from help.

Although the Bible doesn't directly forbid gambling, it's a straightforward matter to find principles in scripture that point the Christian away from it. But the same encouragement exists for you as it does for any other addict. With help from a Christian counselor or addiction treatment program—and from God, of course—an addict committed to the process of recovery can begin to overcome his dependency and rebuild his relationships.

God, somehow I ended up trusting my chances at a casino more than I trusted You. What started as a simple game of chance became an escape from other problems. Of course, what I thought of as an escape was only an attempt to escape, because gambling became a problem that only made my existing problems worse and pushed me further away from You. I felt like a hypocrite for even thinking about looking in Your Word or praying. But I see now that separation from You was not what You wanted but what Satan wanted for me. Deliver me from his lies (and my own). Guide me to the help I need, and help me to restore what I've cost myself and others.

· · ·

Lord, I am desperate for strength to turn from my gambling addiction. I am tired of all the lies I've told myself and others to cover my problem—and of all the justification and rationalization I've used that I called recreation. You are the God of truth, not lies (Isaiah 65:18, Hebrews 6:18), so help me to embrace Your truth. Your Word tells me I should be "strong and courageous. Do not be afraid, for the LORD your God will be with you wherever you go" (Joshua 1:9 NIV). I have a problem, Lord. I need Your help.

Lord God, my gambling is a serious problem. I have gambled without any thought or concern for Your glory, for taking care of my family, for loving my neighbors, or for working for what I need—all things the Bible says a man should do. I have repeatedly tried to get "something for nothing," a sure sign of greed and covetousness, and I have used money to try to accomplish good for myself rather than for Your kingdom. Your Word says, "Whatever does not proceed from faith is sin" (Romans 14:23 ESV). I have sinned. Forgive me, Lord, for trusting odds more than You.

• • •

Father, I'm supposed to live my life depending on You for all I need (Matthew 6:33, Philippians 4:19). I haven't been, though. Instead, my gambling has caused financial hardship for me and my family, with whom I have also broken trust by spending money in casinos that I should have used to care for them. I've ruined my good reputation, and I'm on the verge of despair. I need to stop. Help me want to stop. Give me the guts to confess my sin to my wife and family, to get help, and to find accountability. Help me face the repercussions of my actions and learn what I need to do to follow You and earn back the trust of those I've hurt.

GREED

*Don't be greedy, for a greedy person is an idolater,
worshiping the things of this world.*

COLOSSIANS 3:5 NLT

• • •

Money is a neutral tool, meaning that it can be used for good or evil. So, the real question for us Christians about money is where it ranks in our hearts. We can say God is first, but do our financial records reflect that?

When Jesus talked about having to choose either God or money, He made it clear that our attitude about money boils down to a question of ownership. So who owns your stuff? The Bible says God does: "The earth is the LORD's and the fullness thereof, the world and those who dwell therein" (Psalm 24:1 ESV). So, if you're not an owner, what are you? A steward: "Who is the dependable manager, full of common sense, that the master puts in charge of his staff to feed them well and on time? He is a blessed man if when the master shows up he's doing his job" (Luke 12:42 MSG).

God wants to provide for your needs, but He also wants you to be a conduit of blessing for others—all to the greater glory of His kingdom. With that in mind, you can see that debt, for example, is only symptomatic of the real problem, which is often a heart issue—greed, lack of planning, or failing to put God first.

The world's economy functions on the principle of "too much is never enough," but God's economy is a paradox: generosity leads to blessing, not poverty: "The generous will themselves be blessed, for they share their food with the poor" (Proverbs 22:9 NIV). The true, lasting rewards of good stewardship come after this lifetime, when God rewards those who have done well with what He has given them.

Father, forgive me for the way I have rationalized my focus on getting more and more things. I've put keeping up with the Joneses ahead of keeping my eyes on You—and I've tried to justify my acquisitions as by-products of Your blessings. Show me the real problem behind my behavior, no matter how hard it is for me to learn. My desire for things has alienated me from You, and it has kept me from being the person You made me to be: a source of blessing, not merely a receptacle.

● ● ●

Lord, my greed has disguised itself as good, but everything I get leaves me feeling unsatisfied—and I realize that's not Your best for me. I've found myself thinking, I deserve that or If I don't get this, I'll be missing out. Forgive me for thinking of You as my genie instead of my God. I want to honor You by representing You well in every part of my life, especially my finances.

Jesus, protect my heart against serving myself with my money instead of You. You made it clear that You expect a return on Your investment in us (Luke 19)—which shows that money can be used to make a profit without greed. I want to use what You give me to bless my family and my community, to bring people into Your kingdom, and to make my finances part of my witness for Your glory.

. . .

God, I repent of not being content with what You have given me. I've gotten what I want mixed up with what I need, and that's because I've taken my eyes off You and set them on what I think You should provide. Your Word says, "If riches increase, do not set your heart on them" (Psalm 62:10 NKJV). I've made an idol of money, putting it in a higher place in my heart than You. Forgive me, and teach me to be content, to give, and to trust Your provision. I will seek You first.

HELPLESSNESS

"I am the vine; you are the branches.
If you remain in me and I in you, you will bear
much fruit; apart from me you can do nothing."

JOHN 15:5 NIV

• • •

There's no worse feeling for a man than helplessness. Even if we understand that God helps the helpless, the thought of what we could have done differently or failed to do tears us up. Sometimes, fear of failure paralyzes us in the face of difficult circumstances.

Once we're able to admit we need help, and that we should ask God for it, questions remain: How do we get Him to help us? How do we release His power in our lives? Part of the problem is that we don't understand or embrace our role and authority as citizens of God's kingdom. As the church, we are called to spread the gospel and stand against the enemy—and Jesus has given us the authority to do so.

When Jesus said, "He who is in you is greater than he who is in the world" (1 John 4:4 NKJV), He wasn't telling us to go chase whatever dreams caught our fancy, but to stand against false teachers—something that matters a lot to God.

The world system promotes self-sufficiency and self-determination—the captain-of-your-own-destiny thing—all of which is both fleeting and frustrating. But you have a higher calling in Christ. Align your goals with God's and embrace the mandate He has given you to rule well. God has given you the authority to represent Him, and you access His power by living in His will—humbly, responsibly, and with expectancy.

God, I see that the times I feel helpless are the times I haven't understood or acted in the power and authority You have given me as Your son. I may not know the answers to the problems around me, but You do. If I act on my own, my helplessness will increase. But if I act as Your servant and in alignment with Your will (which I know from reading Your Word), You will give me the power I need to do what You want me to do. Your "divine power has given to [me] all things that pertain to life and godliness" (2 Peter 1:3 NKJV).

* * *

Lord, I want to understand the greatness of Your power, which gives me the wisdom and ability I need to accomplish Your will in my life and in the world around me. Your Spirit in me clothes me with Your power to go out and represent You. I ask You for the wisdom to understand and access "the exceeding greatness of [Your] power toward us who believe" (Ephesians 1:19 NKJV), the same power that raised Christ from the dead and set Him above all things. That's the power in me to be the man You've called me to be.

Jesus, release me from these feelings of helplessness. I want to be the man You've called me to be, and I want to live under Your authority just as You lived under the Father's while You were on earth. Forgive me for any lack of obedience, for any desire to choose my way over Yours, so that I can fulfill Your promise that "anyone who believes in me will do the same works I have done, and even greater works" (John 14:12 NLT).

• • •

God, I'm done with this learned helplessness in my life. My unbelief has compromised Your authority and power in my life. There have been times when I didn't see You working in my life or in the world around me, and I assumed that, because I couldn't see it, You wouldn't work or You didn't care. Help my unbelief (Mark 9:24), cast out my fear with Your perfect love (1 John 4:18), and cleanse me of rebellious thoughts (Psalm 51:10). Jesus said, "As the Father sent me, even so I am sending you" (John 20:21 ESV). Here I am.

• • •

Father, Your Word says, "The helpless commits himself to You; You are the helper of the fatherless" (Psalm 10:14 NKJV). I feel like there's no way out of the situation I'm in, but I know that nothing is impossible for You. As the psalmist prayed, "My help comes from the LORD, the Maker of heaven and earth" (Psalm 121:2 NIV). I am not trapped, and I am not helpless because I am Yours.

HIDDEN SIN

How can I know all the sins lurking in my heart?
Cleanse me from these hidden faults.

PSALM 19:12 NLT

• • •

Beginning back in the Garden of Eden, men have tried to hide from the reality of sin and its consequences. We blame-shift, call it something else, or pretend it's no big deal. But we can feel the nudging of the Holy Spirit, calling it what it is: sin. Be grateful for those little taps on the shoulder of your conscience, for they are signs that God is trying to remind you of who you are, His redeemed son and co-heir with Christ.

You're God's son, but as long as you live in this particular version of your body, you'll wrestle with its baser impulses (Romans 7). At the same time, though, it's futile to try to ignore your sin. If King David couldn't get away with it (2 Samuel 11, Psalms 32 and 51), neither will you. As the apostle Paul wrote, "Don't be misled: No one makes a fool of God. What a person plants, he will harvest. The person who plants selfishness, ignoring the needs of others—ignoring God!—harvests a crop of weeds. All he'll have to show for his life is weeds! But the one who plants in response to God, letting God's Spirit do the growth work in him, harvests a crop of real life, eternal life" (Galatians 6:7–8 MSG).

So, if there's anything you feel you need to hide, be careful because sin is most likely in play. Whatever you're hiding is not God's best for you.

Lord, "When I kept silent, my bones wasted away through my groaning all day long. . . .Then I acknowledged my sin to you and did not cover up my iniquity" (Psalm 32:3, 5 NIV). David's confession convicts me. Thank You for forgiving me. Teach me Your ways.

* * *

God, I want to see my sin the way You do—as something that keeps me from a closer relationship with You. When I think about it like that, it seems silly to try to hide anything from You. I turn from that kind of thinking and invite You to inspect me closely. Show me anything that might create distance between us. I will confess it and repent.

God, be merciful to me. I look inside myself and see so many shadows. I'm grateful that they stand out in contrast to the light of Your Spirit in me, convicting me of my sin. Cleanse me and fill me with Your Spirit, so that I won't keep sinning against You.

• • •

Father, my sin has found me out (Numbers 32:23), as it always does. I hid it from others, but not from You. I'm ashamed and embarrassed for thinking I could get away with it, for imagining I could hide anything from You—for even wanting to hide anything from You. Thank You for Your promise: "If we confess our sins, he is faithful and just to forgive us our sins and to cleanse us from all unrighteousness" (1 John 1:9 ESV).

HOPELESSNESS

"Now is your time of grief, but I will see you again and you will rejoice, and no one will take away your joy."

JOHN 16:22 NIV

• • •

Loss of hope is dangerous. Frustration and hardship can build up, and, without relief, they will strip us of our belief that God is involved in our lives in good and caring ways. But take this to heart: even though your life circumstances are real and difficult, they do not negate God's existence, presence, or providence.

Paul, in seeking to spread the good news of Christ, faced just about every hardship imaginable—imprisonment, beatings, betrayal, slander, shipwreck, abandonment—but he let the peace of God guard his heart (Philippians 4:7). He said, "I have learned in whatever situation I am to be content" (v. 11 ESV).

While there's a time to lament life's tribulations (preferably in the company of a friend or counselor who understands the ministry of just being there), there's also a time to take an inward look at why we feel hopeless. So much of our loss of hope hinges on our discontentment with our lives as they are. For example, single Christians look at married people and wish they were married too, and married believers look at single people and wish they were unmarried. Some find their jobs lacking, their churches unsatisfying, or their communities disappointing.

Sometimes, in extreme cases of hopelessness, believers look at their lives and think it would just be easier to end them.

But here's the thing: changing your circumstances isn't always the answer; sometimes, changing your outlook is. Look past the lies that God doesn't care or that you deserve better. God has already given you His best—His Son, Jesus Christ—and in Him, you have everything you need to live a satisfying, godly life. When you see what God has done for you as ultimately good, contentment will follow, and He will give you the joy you need to hope again. Cry out to Him in your anguish and know that He is listening.

Jesus, nothing in the Bible tells me to ask only when I feel hopeful or strong or capable; there's only the instruction to ask. Ask, You said, and it will be given (Matthew 7:7). You didn't say what would be given, or how, or when—all the things I feel would give me hope. But You told me to ask, and that means You care about what I want and need. The rest I leave to You: "And now, O Lord, for what do I wait? My hope is in you" (Psalm 39:7 ESV).

· · ·

Father, You love me with an everlasting love (Jeremiah 31:3). Nothing can separate me from Your love, "Not trouble, not hard times, not hatred, not hunger, not homelessness, not bullying threats, not backstabbing, not even the worst sins listed in Scripture. . . .None of this fazes us because Jesus loves us" (Romans 8:35, 37 MSG). Your love is my hope and peace and joy.

Lord, I'm having a hard time seeing any of the great plans Your Word says You have for me. My life has not gone the way I had hoped and prayed it would, and I can feel the anger and frustration giving way to despair. As David prayed, "You know how I am scorned, disgraced and shamed; all my enemies are before you. . . .I looked for sympathy, but there was none, for comforters, but I found none" (Psalm 69:19–20 NIV). Don't hide from me, Lord! I need You.

* * *

God, I've run into so many dead ends lately. I've made some bad decisions, and others have made decisions that affected me negatively. My trust has been betrayed, so I feel like I'm going out on a limb to say this: I trust that what is impossible with me is possible with You (Luke 18:27). Because of Jesus, I "have this hope as an anchor for the soul, firm and secure" (Hebrews 6:19 NIV).

INFERTILITY

Take delight in the LORD, and he will give you your heart's desires. Commit everything you do to the LORD. Trust him, and he will help you.

PSALM 37:4–5 NLT

• • •

If you and your wife are facing infertility, it's easy to feel helpless. But you have more power than you realize. As the spiritual leader of your family, you have the authority and power to access God in prayer. Covering your wife in prayer in such a heartbreaking situation is critical to her comfort and security. In prayer, you can carry the burden with her. She will find comfort in your faith—not because it will necessarily change your circumstances (not that it *won't* either!), but because she's never needed you to be her husband and caretaker more.

Make sure your wife knows she isn't letting you down, and don't take her frustration or anger personally. Let her get her feelings out. And if you are the one who is infertile, it's natural to feel angry and frustrated. Just take care to channel those feelings into prayer and not into harsh words with your wife or others. If you need counsel to move through the situation, get it. The shame you're feeling may be natural, but you are still the leader of your family, still a son of God, still a husband to a wife who needs you more than ever.

Lord God, I think of biblical examples of people who brought their infertility before You and You gave them a child: Isaac and Rebekah (Genesis 25:21), Jacob and Rachel (Genesis 30:22–4), and Elkanah and Hannah (1 Samuel 1:27), to name a few. Add our names to that list, Lord. What odds are too great for You?

• • •

Father, I want to carry my wife's burden in this hard time. I can't do anything about whether or not we have a child; that's up to You. Strengthen me when I'm exhausted and discouraged, and empower me to love her and show her grace. And by Your Spirit, lessen those burdens on her heart.

• • •

God, I am hurt and angry at my inability to help create a baby. My manhood has never felt so assaulted. I need Your help to deal with these feelings in a healthy way. The last thing I want to do is hurt my wife further by taking out my frustrations on her. It's just hard to talk about, so I'm bringing my pain to You.

Lord, I never thought my wife and I would be unable to conceive our own children. There are so many dreams tied up in trying to obey You by being fruitful and multiplying—names we picked, characteristics we hoped they'd inherit (and others they wouldn't), things they'd accomplish, and adventures we'd have together. It hurts so much that it's hard to even think about it. Comfort us in our sorrow.

• • •

Father, You know we'd love to have a child. I am fighting feelings of incompleteness and inability at the thought of our infertility. You are in control, though, and I trust You. I am trying to bear in mind that I am complete in Christ—that when I face a test of faith like this, it produces perseverance, and perseverance produces maturity. Give me the courage to let it do its work so I continue to grow in Christ (James 1:2–4).

INJUSTICE

We are hard-pressed on every side, yet not crushed; we are perplexed, but not in despair; persecuted, but not forsaken; struck down, but not destroyed. . . .For we who live are always delivered to death for Jesus' sake, that the life of Jesus also may be manifested in our mortal flesh.

2 CORINTHIANS 4:8–9, 11 NKJV

• • •

To feel the sting of injustice is to align yourself with God's distaste for dishonesty, oppression, bondage, partiality, abuse, and chaos: "Righteousness and justice are the foundation of your throne; steadfast love and faithfulness go before you" (Psalm 89:14 ESV).

When you look at the headlines, it's easy to shift your anger and thirst for justice to the troublemakers—the terrorists, politicians, and corporations—and fail to recognize yourself as being a part of the problem. After all, because of the Fall, we are all sinners, all capable of extremism and hypocrisy and selfishness in our own ways. You want the perpetrators to get what they deserve, but you shouldn't forget that you deserve justice too.

Embracing grace doesn't mean we shouldn't stand against evil. In fact, the Bible calls us to do both. But don't lose sight of the real enemies: the sin-broken flesh and the devil-dominated system of worldly affairs.

Jesus is coming back, and when He does, He will fix what's broken—but only He is truly righteous and just. Only when we align our view of the world with His—broken and hurting but redeemable and restorable—can we properly engage in the fight against injustice. Rather than taking an *us vs. them* attitude, embrace the complexity of living in a diverse world and represent the God who gave Himself on the Cross for all of us in an act of monumental injustice that birthed the possibility of justice for all.

Jesus, I want to value each person the way You do—especially those society tends to ignore, but also those society tends to hate. Even though Your image has become obscured in all of us, I want to look for it in everyone I meet. I may not be able to see it, but only You can know men's hearts with certainty. It's my job to humble myself, learn about others' needs, and ask to see them through Your eyes. Let me help where I can.

• • •

Father, my heart hurts when I look at all the pain and suffering in the world. I want to help, to make some kind of difference for Your glory and for the increase of Your kingdom, but I don't know where to start. The need is overwhelming, but turning away is not an option. Help me see what's getting in my way—being too busy, fear of the messiness of other people's lives, lack of skills, whatever it may be—and then help me keep my eyes on You as You call me to get involved.

• • •

God, forgive me for my self-righteousness. I have looked at all the trouble in the world and said, like a certain Pharisee, "Thank You that I'm not as bad as that guy" (Luke 18:10–14). But while I may not be as badly behaved as some, without the blood of Christ, I am just as bad off as anyone. We've all fallen short of Your standard; we all need a Savior. I need You, God. As Your son, I want to get involved in the family business—the good and just work You are doing to restore life and renew hope in individual hearts and across the world. Help me to look past all the injustice and offer hope in a just day to come.

Lord, as I look at a world that both fascinates and infuriates me, I'm torn about how to respond. But then I remember that You called me to fight injustice with mercy and righteousness: "Religion that is pure and undefiled before God the Father is this: to visit orphans and widows in their affliction, and to keep oneself unstained from the world" (James 1:27 ESV). Keep the world and all its sin from staining me with hatred and fear. Touch my heart about the things You want me to act on, and give me the heart to love others like You do.

• • •

Lord, true justice flows from Your heart and character. You want my faith in You to be marked by my concern for the things that matter to You—seeking the lost, freeing the oppressed, helping the helpless. I'm up against systems and institutions and policies that are too big and powerful for me, but You've called me to stand in Your strength, using Your tools. Help me to live by these words from the apostle Paul: "The world is unprincipled. It's dog-eat-dog out there! The world doesn't fight fair. But we don't live or fight our battles that way—never have and never will. The tools of our trade aren't for marketing or manipulation, but they are for demolishing that entire massively corrupt culture. We use our powerful God-tools for smashing warped philosophies, tearing down barriers erected against the truth of God, fitting every loose thought and emotion and impulse into the structure of life shaped by Christ. Our tools are ready at hand for clearing the ground of every obstruction and building lives of obedience into maturity" (2 Corinthians 10:3–6 MSG).

INSOMNIA

For to set the mind on the flesh is death,
but to set the mind on the Spirit is life and peace.
ROMANS 8:6 ESV

• • •

You've tossed and turned for what seems like hours. You stayed up late, hoping to wear out your body so you can get to sleep, but your mind just won't shut down for the night. Insomnia takes a toll on every level—physical, emotional, and spiritual.

The inability to sleep can come from a number of causes: medical or health issues, seasons of stress, bad dreams, or hidden sin (see David's take on that in Psalms 32 and 51), for starters. If you've consulted your doctor about physical causes, you probably have an idea what you need to do to sleep better. But the physical is intertwined with the emotional and spiritual.

Think about God, even as you lie in bed. Prayer brings your sleeplessness before your Maker. Ask Him to show you the root cause of your insomnia, and then give Him the issue at hand—worries, anxieties, or even sin. Meditate on His promises to provide for you, and trust Him to strengthen you for the day ahead.

God, there is no shortage of things to worry about. So much of it centers on what I need to get to live a good life—getting enough to pay the bills, put food on the table, deal with medical conditions, advance at work—but it's possible that I've lost sight of all You have already given me and will continue to give me— abundant life, the Holy Spirit, an important ongoing mission, and the promise of heaven, for starters. Help me to focus on You now and leave the rest to You.

• • •

Lord, I don't understand why I can't get to sleep. If I need to clear my conscience of anything, please show me, whether it's sin or bad decisions or anxiety or worry. Whatever it is, I will confess it and repent of it, trusting Your promise to hear and forgive me (1 John 1:9). If I'm guilty, guide me in finding a way to make things right.

Jesus, I ask for Your peace tonight. Your Word says to be
"anxious for nothing, but in everything by prayer and supplication,
with thanksgiving, let your requests be made known to God"
(Philippians 4:6 NKJV). I will think of things that are noble, just,
true, pure, lovely, of good report, virtuous, and praiseworthy
(v. 8). You are the God who never sleeps (Psalm 121:4).
Guard my heart and mind with thoughts of You.

• • •

Lord God, You are my protector, "a shield around me" (Psalm 3:3 NIV).
I have a million reasons not to sleep tonight, and only one reason
to rest: You. Teach me to be content whether I sleep or just rest
tonight, trusting that You will provide all I need to get through my
day tomorrow: "I've learned by now to be quite content whatever
my circumstances. I'm just as happy with little as with much, with
much as with little. I've found the recipe for being happy whether
full or hungry, hands full or hands empty. Whatever I have,
wherever I am, I can make it through anything in the One who
makes me who I am" (Philippians 4:12–13 MSG).

JOB LOSS

*And my God will meet all your needs according
to the riches of his glory in Christ Jesus.*

PHILIPPIANS 4:19 NIV

• • •

Losing a job creates more than financial strain for a man. It undermines the pillars on which we build our identity. What you do, what you know, who you know, and what you have are all subject for reconsideration when you're between jobs. All the hours you put in, all the connections you cultivate, all the information and experience you gain, and all the things your job afforded you to have pile up into what seems like an insurmountable mess.

Unemployment is a time to check and reassess (or reaffirm) your priorities. Look at those identifiers in the light of your relationship with God. You know the Creator of the universe and everything in it, and He wants you to come to Him as your Father. Your highest goal in life is to know Him. Through His Word, you know His will and ways. Everything you do and go through is part of His overarching plan to work all things together. "Yet you, LORD, are our Father. We are the clay, you are the potter; we are all the work of your hand" (Isaiah 64:8 NIV). He will provide for You in this difficult time, and He'll also comfort you as you regroup.

Lord, I am stunned at what has happened. Losing this job just blindsided me, and I'm feeling so many different emotions— hurt, anger, disappointment, and fear among them. I don't know what You are doing by allowing this to happen, but I trust You to help provide for me and my family while this season endures. I commit to keeping my eyes on You, giving You everything I'm feeling, and expecting You to make something good out of this. I need You more than ever.

• • •

God, I've started to see how much value I put on the job I've lost. I've felt worthless, unsure of who I am, and in complete agreement with Solomon: " 'Everything is meaningless,' says the Teacher, 'completely meaningless!' " (Ecclesiastes 1:2 NLT). I've wondered how this could be Your plan for me. But I understand that Your ways and thoughts are higher than mine (Isaiah 55:8–9), and I'm beginning to grasp that this is part of what You meant when You said you are working "all things" together for my good. I guess all things means all things. I want to get onboard with what You're doing and learn what You're trying to teach me during this downtime. My worth is not in my work but in You.

Father, even in this time of loss, I have so much to thank You for—
beginning with Jesus Christ, my Savior. Jesus died for me before
I was even born, but You knew me even then, knew the blessings
You would give me, and knew the challenges You would allow to
help me depend on Your provision. Even though I liked my job, I
love You more. I know You will take care of me and my family.

• • •

God, give me wisdom as I begin my new job of looking for a new
job. I want to be faithful as I make financial adjustments during this
time. I need to think creatively, so please open my mind to learning
new skills and to meeting new people, as well as making the most
of any old connections. My family needs me to lead them spiritually,
even if I'm not providing financially. There is more at stake here
than just finding a job. This is one of the hardest things I've ever
been through, but I choose to do it in a way that honors You.

JOB STRESS

"I've told you all this so that trusting me, you will be unshakable and assured, deeply at peace. In this godless world you will continue to experience difficulties. But take heart! I've conquered the world."

JOHN 16:33 MSG

• • •

Jesus promised us His authority and power in our work in the world, but He never said we'd live stress-free lives. In fact, as He told His disciples about His coming death—an event that would turn their worlds (and the world in general) upside down—He promised two things: they would experience tribulation, and He had conquered the world that would threaten them (John 16:33).

Stress happens, but you don't have to react to it the way everyone else does. If you are truly committed to following Christ in every area of your life, stress and challenges still won't always be easy to deal with, but you will begin to see them as opportunities to represent God well as you show the world the difference your faith makes. And you don't need to stress about that, either, because the Holy Spirit will give you the power to do so, the words to say, and the heart to seek the highest good for those with whom you work.

Make sure the things you're doing at work line up with God's plans and priorities for you. That includes life-work balance, resting and recharging, not overextending yourself (which amounts to doing things in your own strength), and reserving time to build relationships at work and at home.

Remember, these are not the world's priorities, and you will probably face some pushback at work. But if you are seeking God, taking time to be still before Him, and acknowledging Him in all you do, your path will be much clearer and your stress will be more manageable.

God, work is so stressful right now that I can't think straight.
I want to follow Your priorities, no matter what's going on at
work. If my work feels meaningless, You can give meaning to
what I do when I do it for You. If I place too much of my self-worth
on my job, help me find my true identity in You as the son You
love and a servant working toward kingdom goals. I will keep
perspective on the chaos at work by reminding myself
that everything I do is to be done ultimately for You.

• • •

Jesus, You're my real boss. You love me, You're for me, and You
understand me (Colossians 3:23–24). I want Your priorities and
values to inform how I operate at work. As Your representative,
I commit to being the best worker I can be—diligent, prompt,
reliable, organized, and relational—and to seeking the highest
good of the people with whom I work. Guide me as I face
difficult situations and relationships at work.

Lord, I realize that a lot of my stress at work comes from not taking time to rest and recharge. Forgive me for not observing any kind of a Sabbath—a rest period where I just slow down, shift gears, and trust You to provide the energy and ability to do what needs to be done when I go back to work. I will be deliberate about taking time off to recharge.

. . .

Father, work has been extra stressful recently. There are different reasons for it, but I want to keep my eyes on You. I don't want to respond to stress by complaining, speaking in anger, or coping in unhealthy ways like eating junk food, drinking, or binge-watching TV. I'm grateful that You have given me a job, and I want to honor You by doing it the best I can. The way I handle hardship is part of my witness (2 Corinthians 12:8–10). You're the One I don't want to disappoint.

. . .

Lord, I want to handle my job stress in ways that please You. While I would love to do work that allows me to use the gifts and talents You've given me, I trust that You can still use me in positive ways in my current job. Keep my focus on the opportunity You've given me to provide for me and my family. Help me to recognize all the personal, petty, political quarrels that people get into at work and to avoid them. I don't know if it's possible for me to truly enjoy this job, but I know that nothing is impossible for You. As long as You have me there, I will look to honor You with my work.

LEADERSHIP

Be diligent to present yourself approved to God,
a worker who does not need to be ashamed,
rightly dividing the word of truth.

2 Timothy 2:15 NKJV

. . .

Here is a simple but profound truth: you are a leader. You may think you're not, but if you are a Christian, God has called you to follow Christ and to lead others to Him. There are a variety of ways you can do that, and they have nothing to do with being an employer or a manager. No matter who you are or where you work, you're a leader. Even if you're not a husband or a father, you're a leader. If you don't have a college degree or a ton of work experience, you're still a leader. That's because God has called you as a believer to join in His work, the family business of sharing the Gospel and making disciples.

Following Jesus' example, you lead not by lording it over others but by getting low—by humbling yourself to serve in the best way you can. That starts by getting into God's Word daily and learning about Him and what matters to Him—and then putting it into practice.

You'll need to pray and be in fellowship with other like-minded Christian men, because the more you learn about God, the more you learn about yourself—your strengths and weaknesses, what it's like to be on the other side of you, and how to die to yourself so you can become more and more like Jesus. The kingdom of God needs you to embrace your leadership role, to avoid passivity, and to begin ministering where you are, right now.

Lord, I am tired of feeling ineffective and incapable of leadership. I want to accomplish Your purposes for my life and through my life in the lives of others. I want to model what it is to follow Christ, to humble myself and "go low" in prayer and service. I trust that You can use me right where I am.

• • •

God, considering all I have accomplished at work, it seems like I have no real influence or credibility on a personal level. For too long, I've written it off as the jealousy of others, or excused it as not mattering since I produce results. But as a Christian, I am called to a higher purpose than making something that will fade with time—or as soon as I move on or retire. I have acted religious but rejected the power that can make me truly godly (2 Timothy 3:5). I want more—I want what You have for me. I need to put aside any instincts to control or compete or manipulate others to get what I want. I need to model integrity and righteousness, earning the right to instruct and even confront others by showing them that I care about them as people first.

Father, I've invested so much time and energy into serving myself—building up my reputation and my résumé—that I've forgotten that I am to represent You in all I do and say. I've been shortsighted, lacking self-awareness and avoiding God-awareness. Forgive me. I want to embrace the greater role You have for me as a follower of Christ and as a fisher of men. I desire to be someone who wants to see the boundaries and population of Your kingdom expand. Let me use the gifts You've given me to lead others in exercising their gifts.

• • •

Lord, I realize that I have been passive in my leadership role. I'm beginning to see the cost of my inability and unwillingness to get involved or to confront problems or take stands on important issues. I've excused it as just being humble or meek, which You've called me to be, but I see that my version of those things is very different from Jesus' demonstration of those qualities. He told the truth—sometimes through stories, sometimes directly—but He always sought Your will and Your best in the lives of the people He encountered. Help me to love others like that, at home and at work.

LITIGATION

The king's heart is a stream of water in the hand
of the Lord; he turns it wherever he will.

Proverbs 21:1 esv

· · ·

Whatever legal justification may exist for filing a lawsuit, the Bible calls Christians to avoid suing each other. Jesus laid out principles for resolving conflict between two Christians (Matthew 18:15–20). Paul called believers to task for making God's church look bad by taking each other to court over petty issues (1 Corinthians 6:1–8) and instructed us that, "so far as it depends on you, live peaceably with all" (Romans 12:18 esv).

The legal system is adversarial in nature, and God wants us to live in unity with our brothers and sisters and civilly with those who don't believe. However, there are times when you find yourself facing a lawsuit. It's an alarming, frightening situation, and you have to respond whether or not you like it. If another believer is bringing the suit, appeal to him as a fellow Christian to sit down with you and work it out. If it's a non-believer, you can exercise without guilt your legal right to defend yourself. In either case, check your heart against God's Word (Proverbs 6:16–19 is a good guide) because how you handle the situation is part of your witness as a follower of Christ. Beyond your fear, anger, and lack of certainty, trust God to do right without partiality (Genesis 18:25).

God, You are my heavenly Father and my Lord, but You are also my Judge. There is no favoritism with You (Romans 2:11), and You are perfect and just in all Your ways (2 Samuel 22:31). You know whether I have been justly named in this lawsuit. I believe that I have not, and I plead my case before You. Deliver me, according to Your righteous nature and judgment. I hold on to Your Word: "The Lord will fight for you, and you have only to be silent" (Exodus 14:14 ESV).

. . .

Father, the pressure and uncertainty of this lawsuit is crushing my spirit and sickening my body. I am trying to represent You as I face it, but I believe the suit has no legal merit. Please get it dismissed in whatever way You choose. You are my strength and my shield (Psalm 28:7), and You have said that no weapon formed against me shall succeed (Isaiah 54:17).

*Lord, as I face this unjust lawsuit, Your Word gives me peace:
"If anyone attacks you, don't for a moment suppose that I sent
them, and if any should attack, nothing will come of it. I create the
blacksmith who fires up his forge and makes a weapon designed to
kill. I also create the destroyer—but no weapon that can hurt you
has ever been forged. Any accuser who takes you to court will be
dismissed as a liar. This is what God's servants can expect. I'll see
to it that everything works out for the best" (Isaiah 54:15–17 MSG).*

* * *

*Lord, my case is coming up and my stomach is tied in knots. Your
Word says I will reap what I have sown (Galatians 6:7–8), and I
acknowledge that I am facing the consequences of my actions.
Only You know whether I will go free or face punishment. I confess
my sins before You, and I turn from them. I ask You to deliver
me from this, Lord. I commit to being the man and citizen You
have called me to be. I leave all this in Your hands, but pray that
whether or not I go free, You would free me in Jesus Christ.*

MARITAL STRIFE/DYSFUNCTION

"So then, they are no longer two but one flesh. Therefore what God has joined together, let not man separate."

MATTHEW 19:6 NKJV

* * *

When you said "I do," the last thing you were thinking of was conflict with your beloved. But conflict is a reality, even in the best of relationships. That doesn't mean your relationship is doomed, although if you don't get to the core issues and work on resolving them, the bumpy parts of the ride can seem unending.

If either you or your wife thought you were marrying a perfect person, you were entering marriage with your eyes half-shut. Before you got married, you probably found your differences complementary. Now, however, they've somehow become problematic. But it's not that either of you has suddenly swapped personalities; you've just changed your perspective, realizing that it's challenging to live day in and day out with another person.

Check your expectations. Are they realistic? Does your wife think so? Measure your behavior against Paul's instruction: "Let each one of you love his wife as himself, and let the wife see that she respects her husband" (Ephesians 5:33 ESV). Invite conversation instead of confrontation and common ground rather than criticism. Learn to live with each other with understanding and appreciation for the work God is doing in each of you—and how He is using each of you to teach the other to die to yourselves. God's design for marriage includes unique blessings of intimacy that mirror the profound depth of Christ's relationship with the church. It's worth fighting for.

God, You made me and my wife one flesh (Genesis 2:24)—joined in
every way: emotionally, physically, spiritually, financially. But lately
we can't seem to stop treating each other like the enemy. I feel
disrespected, but I admit that I have not loved her like Christ loved
the church. We both think we're right, but that creates conflict, so
we're also both wrong. I'm struggling to be open, to give her the
benefit of the doubt. Forgive me, and make me into the husband
You want her to have. Help us to find godly counsel and good
friends with whom we can share our journey.

• • •

Lord, Your Word says love "always protects, always trusts,
always hopes, always perseveres" (1 Corinthians 13:7 NIV).
You've called me to love my wife no matter how she responds,
but I see that if I love her the way I'm supposed to, she is
much more likely to respond in positive ways.

Father, guide me in loving my wife the way You've called me to—sacrificially. Although she is my wife, she has always been Your daughter. I want to love her in a way that honors You. That includes fighting for her best interests because they are tied to mine. Keep chipping away at me so that more and more of You is revealed. Help us to learn and grow from those conflicts, becoming better off, not bitter.

• • •

God, please bless my marriage. I understand that when I draw closer to You, and my wife does the same, we grow closer together. Show me the negativity in my heart—anything that keeps me from showing patience, forgiveness, kindness, and affection toward my wife. Give me the wisdom I need to distinguish between faults and sins, and to strive for resolution when there's a conflict. Help me learn when to give way and when to hold the line. I commit to listening twice as much as I speak—and listening well. I commit to being responsible in my devotion to You, regularly spending time in Your Word and in prayer so I can know what kind of man You want me to be. Make my marriage like a full moon, a beautiful reflection of the Son.

Father, we keep running into the same obstacles in our marriage and having the same kinds of fights. We trust that You have more for us, and that You can use each of us to smooth out the other's rough spots. My wife is worth fighting for. I want to share Paul's attitude about hardship: "We can rejoice, too, when we run into problems and trials, for we know that they help us develop endurance. And endurance develops strength of character, and character strengthens our confident hope of salvation. And this hope will not lead to disappointment. For we know how dearly God loves us, because he has given us the Holy Spirit to fill our hearts with his love" (Romans 5:3–5 NLT).

• • •

Lord, Your Word says that a wife should submit to her husband "as to the Lord" (Ephesians 5:22 ESV). I confess, however, that I have used that verse to make demands of my wife but have conveniently ignored the verses close by on either side of it: "Husbands, love your wives, as Christ loved the church and gave himself up for her" (v. 25) and the call to be "submitting to one another out of reverence for Christ" (v. 21). So, I submit to You, asking You to help me love my wife like You love the church—giving up all I am for her and seeking to help her know You better. Forgive me, and help me to become the man she needs.

PORNOGRAPHY

*Run from sexual sin! No other sin so clearly
affects the body as this one does. For sexual
immorality is a sin against your own body.*

1 CORINTHIANS 6:18 NLT

· · ·

Erotic images make us feel powerful and in control—but these sensations are fleeting and false. Porn is like a gateway drug that causes hormones in key areas of your brain, areas God intended for pleasure with your wife, to be dispersed among a panorama of images, numbing the sensations so that the regular viewer must constantly seek more lurid content to get the same "high." It's a self-made trap.

The Bible tells us as much: "For all that *is* in the world—the lust of the flesh, the lust of the eyes, and the pride of life—is not of the Father but is of the world. And the world is passing away, and the lust of it" (1 John 2:16–17 NKJV). Giving yourself over to those lusts weakens your walk with Christ, darkening your mind with depravity (Romans 1:28). Lust also destroys unity with your wife and diminishes your view of women in general.

But God has provided a way out. It begins with repentance—turning away from your porn habit. This may mean getting filters for your devices or even abandoning the internet if need be. It means disciplining yourself in studying God's Word, renewing your mind (Romans 12:1–2). Every time you feel like viewing the bad stuff, go to the Bible instead and fill your mind with the good stuff. Finally, you need accountability. This is the hardest part for most guys, but it's important to bring your private life into the light. Find at least one other male believer and tell him about your porn use. Have him check in with you regularly (maybe daily at first, then weekly). If you're serious about breaking free from lust, God will use these practices to liberate you.

God, thank You that Your Word says that "he who does the will of God abides forever" (1 John 2:17 NKJV). I have sought my own will, my own pleasure, for far too long, and I can feel the distance it has created between me and You. As I seek You in prayer and in Your Word, deliver me from pornography's grip and from the lust of my heart. You are stronger than my sin. Give me strength to resist as I replace my thoughts with Your thoughts.

• • •

Jesus, You warned us about looking at the wrong things: "The eye is the lamp of the body. If your eyes are healthy, your whole body will be full of light. But if your eyes are unhealthy, your whole body will be full of darkness. If then the light within you is darkness, how great is that darkness!" (Matthew 6:22–23 NIV). Pierce my darkness, Lord. Turn my eyes toward You, Your Word and ways, so that I can win the battle in my mind's eye.

Lord, my porn use has damaged intimacy between me and my wife. I've objectified women for my own pleasure for so long that I have forgotten what it means to share real intimacy with the one woman You intended for me to be with. Help me as I confess my sin to her and seek help to get us back on the right path. Teach me again what it means to share intimacy, and help me to have honest, open conversations with my wife about our needs. Help me to be patient as I rebuild trust with her.

• • •

Father, meet me in the midst of my failure. I've tried to stay pure and fallen again. The weight of my sin is especially heavy right now. I don't understand how You can keep loving me when I hate myself so much. This is the enemy's tactic, though—lust or loathing, I lose and he's happy. I'm desperate for relief. Get this out of me! Your Word reminds me that "godly grief produces a repentance that leads to salvation without regret, whereas worldly grief produces death" (2 Corinthians 7:10 ESV). The devil may have won this battle, but he won't keep me from throwing myself on Your mercy. This prayer of brokenness is my act of hope. I will keep breathing, keep fighting, keep hoping in You. Save me, Lord!

PRODIGAL CHILDREN

Though the fig tree does not bud and there are no grapes on the
vines, though the olive crop fails and the fields produce no food,
though there are no sheep in the pen and no cattle in the stalls,
yet I will rejoice in the LORD, I will be joyful in God my Savior.
HABAKKUK 3:17–18 NIV

• • •

Stress is a part of family life, and leading your family with Joshua 24:15 determination does not exempt you from it. Some family stress comes as a result of men not leading their families in the fear and admonition of the Lord (Ephesians 6:4). But sometimes, you and your wife can seek the Lord in all you do and still hit a brick wall with your kids and face a dark, unexpected season of hardship.

Issues like who does what chore and how much time should be spent on the computer are common annoyances that can be handled without too much disruption, but what about when your kids fall away from the faith you've raised them in? Or when your son informs you that he's not the gender he was born as? What happens when your little girl comes home a week after her sweet sixteenth and tells you she's pregnant? God doesn't guarantee a smooth ride, but He does promise to be with you through whatever you're facing.

Let your kids know that you've set boundaries for everyone's safety and security, but also let them know that you love them no matter what—that even if you don't like their choices, you will never stop loving them. Do what you can, then let God do His work in their lives. He is faithful to finish what He started.

Lord God, sometimes I feel like I'm trapped in a prison with my family. We're prisoners of bad choices and crushing consequences, but I pray that I would be able to lead us, even as we're in this dark place. Let Paul's words inspire and comfort me: "I am suffering here in prison. But I am not ashamed of it, for I know the one in whom I trust, and I am sure that he is able to guard what I have entrusted to him until the day of his return" (2 Timothy 1:12 NLT). I won't give up because You won't.

• • •

God, I feel like my children have changed but I haven't. Despite the way my wife and I raised our kids, the world got its teeth into them, and it feels like they've been poisoned against us and, worse yet, against You. I feel like I've failed You in the most important job You've given me—being a dad. Remind me that my real goal in life is to know You more. I want to learn whatever it is You're trying to teach me as I deal with my children's choices. I love them and want Your best for them. Help me to love them like You do.

• • •

Father, I thought I was raising arrows to shoot out into the world for Your glory, but I can't even keep them in the quiver properly (Psalm 127:3–5). Even so, Your Word in Habakkuk 3:17–18 points to my relationship with You as my strength when it feels like my family is coming apart at the seams. I will rejoice in You, even when there is little or no evidence of fruit in my children's lives. Lead me so I can know how to love them.

God, I've had such times of joy with my family. Now that we're struggling, let me be like Job and accept the bad from You as well as the good (Job 2:10). I refuse to fall into passivity. Let my family see me walking with You through all this, learning and growing and relying on You. I will act for their good and not to satisfy my ego. I will cover my wife in prayer and listen to her concerns. I will look for the good in my kids even when the bad is right in my face. Keep all our hearts tender toward You and each other.

• • •

Father, please preserve my children as they stray from You. Don't hold against them whatever sins of mine have contributed to their distance from You. Protect them from the worst consequences of their own decisions. I know they will have regrets—I always have when I've strayed from You. At the same time, You have always been faithful to teach me more about Your grace, peace, and love through my mistakes. Please do the same with them. Let me be like the father of the prodigal son, who kept looking down the road in hopes that he would see his son coming home. When that day comes, I will rejoice!

SEXUAL IDENTITY

So now there is no condemnation for those who belong
to Christ Jesus. And because you belong to him,
the power of the life-giving Spirit has freed you
from the power of sin that leads to death.

ROMANS 8:1–2 NLT

• • •

There's a difference between same-sex attraction and committing to a homosexual or transgender lifestyle. The first is a real but misplaced desire that you can give over to God. But actively engaging in a gay or transgender relationship directly violates God's Word (1 Corinthians 6:9–10) and denies His presence and power in your life.

God's Word makes it clear that Christians should encourage anyone who struggles with sin to resist it and to follow Christ's example, rather than join in with piling on with the condemnation. That is in keeping with Christ's example: "For God did not send His Son into the world to condemn the world, but that the world through Him might be saved" (John 3:17 NKJV).

Most homosexuals and people struggling with gender identity have had those feelings for most of their lives, and if they've grown up around the church, they've likely also dealt with feelings of shame, disgust, rejection, and alienation. But the truth is that it's no different for a gay man than it is for any other man tempted by his own desires: he can either choose Christ or himself.

God has good plans for all of us sinners (Jeremiah 29:11), which He can enact in our lives when we give ourselves completely to Him. The person struggling with homosexuality or gender identity needs love and fellowship and discipleship, just like any man does. If this is your struggle, know that Jesus loves you. Let His goodness and mercy lead you to repentance (Romans 2:4) and realize that though your battle won't be easy, God will never give up on you or abandon you.

God, I commit myself to honoring You and to trusting You with my feelings. I pray that You will deliver me from my sinful desires, specifically my attraction to other men. I ask this with all my heart and with expectation. I want to be included with those Paul described this way: "Some of you were once like that. But you were cleansed; you were made holy; you were made right with God by calling on the name of the Lord Jesus Christ and by the Spirit of our God" (1 Corinthians 6:11 NLT).

• • •

Father, I can't deny my feelings, but I know that my behavior is based on a choice I make every day to follow You and flee sexual immorality (1 Corinthians 6:18). Help me resist the desires that are not Your best for me and instead embrace Your holiness, grace, and desire for purity in all my ways—the same things You want from all Your children. Give me Your abundant life (John 10:10).

• • •

Lord, I have prayed hard and often and asked You to take these feelings away from me. But You haven't. Remind me that You still love me, that You still have plans for me. I think of what You told Paul when he begged You to take away his physical suffering: "My grace is all you need. My power works best in weakness" (2 Corinthians 12:9 NLT). I'm grateful that You don't make mistakes, including me, and even though my body doesn't match my desires, same-sex attraction won't separate me from Your love. Strengthen me in my commitment to honoring You.

Jesus, I am struggling with desires that are forbidden in Your Word, and with a culture and world that have put individual freedom as the highest possible good. I confess that sometimes I just want to do what feels right. But I give my feelings to You. I'm made in Your image, and You also made me male. You created sexuality, and You meant for it to be glorious and good, but You set it aside for marriage between a man and a woman. You alone can redeem the brokenness in me and in the world around me. Start with me, Lord. When I'm faced with temptation, let my response be like Yours—to choose the will of the Father above my own.

• • •

Lord, I just found out someone I care about is struggling with his sexuality. My first impulse was to reject him, as if his struggle was somehow unpardonable. Forgive me. We all deal with our flesh and our own battles, and this struggle has got to be so hard for him. Help me to be there for him, to look past the way it makes me feel and do what You've told me to—being there for him and encouraging him to seek Your best for his life, even if it goes against his feelings.

SINGLENESS

But each one has his own gift from God,
one in this manner and another in that.

1 CORINTHIANS 7:7 NKJV

• • •

When God created the first man, He made him single. Later, He designed marriage because it was what He intended for Adam. But while Adam was in both states—married and single—God called what He made "good." So, there's nothing inherently better or worse about either state. Throughout church history, some have favored marriage over singleness, but for the Christian man, staying single or getting married is a matter of where God leads each individual.

Some men desperately want to be married and some don't. Biblically, there are reasons why a person might remain single. In Matthew 19:11–12, Jesus spoke of three types of "eunuchs"—those who stay single and celibate. Some are born "wired" to stay single, some are forced into it by external circumstances (like castration), and some choose it in order to focus wholeheartedly on kingdom work. Whatever the case, singles matter to God, and they need friends and co-laborers as much as anyone else.

Not being married is not a sign of defect, nor is being single indicative of greater holiness than being married. If you're single, don't be in a hurry to get married. Seek God daily to see if He has the right woman for you—or if He wants you to stay single. Also, stay connected at work and church and develop friendships. Christian fellowship should consist of singles and married couples, young and old, and men and women. If God calls you to be single, trust Him to give you the grace to live in it effectively and joyfully.

God, I admit that I often feel lonely as a single man. I try to cultivate friendships with a variety of people, but I look at married couples I know and wonder if You want me to be married. So, in a way, what I'm really feeling is frustration. I'm pretty sure I want to be married, but I have no idea what women want from me. According to Your design, men are to be the spiritual leaders of their families. Guide me as a leader—morally, financially, and spiritually—in all that I'm doing now so that I can find the balance between taking the initiative with women and being passive.

• • •

Father, I am trying to be faithful in everything You've given me to do in my life—my work, ministry, and relationships. I've had relationships with women that seem headed for marriage, but then it didn't work out. I hope it's because we both realized that it was because You didn't have a future for us and not because You really want me to be a monk or something similarly isolating. Guide me on my journey, and keep me from fear. Step by step, let me see You on the path ahead of me so I can know I'm headed in the right direction.

LORD, as I navigate this journey of singleness, Proverbs 18:22 (NKJV) comes up a lot: "He who finds a wife finds a good thing, and obtains favor from the LORD." But then, so do Paul's words: "So I say to those who aren't married and to widows [and, I'm guessing, widowers]—it's better to stay unmarried, just as I am" (1 Corinthians 7:8 NLT). So, there are pros and cons either way. I want to focus on what You have for me now, which appears to be singleness. I'm open to Your leading, but Paul's words give me encouragement: "I want you to live as free of complications as possible. When you're unmarried, you're free to concentrate on simply pleasing the Master" (v. 32 MSG).

• • •

God, being single has its own blessings and challenges, and sex is definitely one of those challenges. Help me to resist this sex-saturated culture—it's even in the church these days!—and not be consumed with my physical urges. Sexuality is only one part of who You made me to be, but it's not the basis of the highest good I could ever experience. Guide me toward other ways I can burn off that energy and be sharpened and encouraged by other Christian single men. Above all, I want to honor You and focus on what You are doing now and not on what I am not experiencing. What looks like "lack" in the world's eyes is an opening to a fruitful life, a life fully committed to You.

Jesus, I commit to truly loving others the way You did. I want to seek the highest good of those You bring into my life, focusing not on the "don'ts" of singleness but the "dos" of following Christ. Help me to maintain appropriate and respectful boundaries in my relationships, especially with women—particularly with emotional intimacy, which, along with physical intimacy, You've reserved for marriage. Let Your Word guide me: "Everyone who believes that Jesus is the Christ has become a child of God. And everyone who loves the Father loves his children, too. We know we love God's children if we love God and obey his commandments" (1 John 5:1–2 NLT).

SURGERY

"I am leaving you with a gift—peace of mind and heart.
And the peace I give is a gift the world cannot give.
So don't be troubled or afraid."

JOHN 14:27 NLT

• • •

Surgery is often a scary proposition. Even when we've had time to prepare, it's hard to go under anesthesia, which might seem like a sneak peek at a peaceful death. Whether it's you or a loved one preparing for an operation, or whether it's planned in advance or needed as an emergency, surgery can be unsettling. No matter the circumstances, though, God is still in control and still very much aware of your circumstances and needs, and He will be with You through it all. Seek Him in the expectation that the operation will accomplish its most hopeful objectives and more—but also in expectation of His peace and presence.

Lord, my loved one is facing surgery. Be his peace right now as You strengthen his body and prepare his mind and spirit. Give his doctors the greatest skill possible and guide the outcome toward the highest possible good. Would You help him to recover quickly and be better off because of this operation? Thank You, Lord, for my dear one. I lift him up to You in Jesus' name.

• • •

Father, there is nowhere I can go where You are not with me (Psalm 139). But I confess I'm feeling nervous before this surgery. Strengthen me in mind, body, and soul to face this. Give my doctors sharp minds and steady hands, and guide them if they come up short. I want to be at my best as soon as possible so I can go on with the work You have for me. You have given me new life in Christ, and You are the healer and sustainer of my soul. Heal my body as well, Father, and glorify Your name in the process.

God, I am leaning into Your arms as I face this operation. Protect me and help this surgery to go well. The thought of You being with me when I am at my weakest gives me comfort. I also ask that You watch over my loved ones and give them a strong sense of Your presence and peace while I'm out. Your Word is my strength: "Do not be anxious about anything, but in everything by prayer and supplication with thanksgiving let your requests be made known to God. And the peace of God, which surpasses all understanding, will guard your hearts and your minds in Christ Jesus" (Philippians 4:6–7 ESV).

* * *

Lord, I face this surgery with expectation, hope, and faith. I'm focused on these words You've given me: "And the prayer offered in faith will make the sick person well; the Lord will raise them up. If they have sinned, they will be forgiven" (James 5:15 NIV). Bring to my mind anything I need to confess and any person with whom I need to make things right, bringing Your healing on a spiritual level in advance of bringing it on a physical one. I put my trust in You.

UNFORGIVENESS

"For if you forgive men their trespasses, your heavenly Father will also forgive you. But if you do not forgive men their trespasses, neither will your Father forgive your trespasses."
MATTHEW 6:14–15 NKJV

• • •

Unforgiveness is like drinking poison and hoping the other person gets sick. Jesus told the story of a king who forgave a huge debt his servant owed him, but the servant refused to forgive those who owed him. When the king found out about this unforgiveness, he sentenced the man to be tortured until he paid every cent (Matthew 18:23–35).

When we refuse to forgive those who have wronged us, we are disobeying God, who has forgiven us the ultimate debt. Even if we don't get tossed to the creditors because of our stubborn hearts, our own bitterness and cynicism will torture us.

Failing to forgive creates a glitch in your relationship with God, and it cuts you off from the mercy you've failed to grant and opens a foothold in your heart for Satan. If you wait until you feel like forgiving someone, you never will, so "submit to God. Resist the devil, and he will flee from you" (James 4:7 NKJV). The Holy Spirit will help you obey God and truly forgive those who have hurt you.

Lord, I have spent too much time keeping accounts of wrong done against me. I felt justified in doing so, but I now understand that I've only been adding to an oppressive weight on my soul. The Bible says vengeance is Yours, and You will pay people back for their wrongdoing—me included (Hebrews 10:30). You have better things for me than paying people back. Forgive me for the energy I've put into my anger and hardheartedness. I will forgive those who have wronged me because You forgave me.

• • •

God, I've struggled to forgive certain people. I've made all sorts of justifications for not doing so, but in the end, I'm just angry and hurt. I can feel my pain growing in me like a weed, though, and I need Your help to root it out. I know that starts with me forgiving those who have hurt me. I'm sorry for forgetting all You have forgiven me for. Forgiveness is based on Your character and the redeeming work of Christ at the Cross. I leave my anger and pain there. Fill the void with Your grace, mercy, and forgiveness, so I can extend to others what You first gave me.

Father, I've been like the Pharisee who criticized Jesus for letting the woman wash his feet with perfume and her hair. He called her a sinner, and Jesus didn't disagree but said, "Her many sins have been forgiven—as her great love has shown. But whoever has been forgiven little loves little" (Luke 7:47 NIV). By Your grace, help me to love my enemies, and so release myself from the bitterness of unforgiveness.

• • •

Jesus, in failing to forgive, I've cut myself off from forgiveness. Your Word says, "Forgive others, and you will be forgiven" (Luke 6:37 NLT). I've been seeing myself as a victim, but that only hurts me and others who have done me no wrong. I'm trusting You that when I do forgive, You'll guide me to the core cause of my stubbornness— self-defense, fear, mistrust, unreasonable expectations, whatever it may be. Bring about fresh starts in these relationships—renewal of trust and reconciliation—and let that start with me.

VIOLENCE

The violence of the wicked sweeps them away,
because they refuse to do what is just.

<small>PROVERBS 21:7 NLT</small>

• • •

The world is full of sin and violence, and it's a challenge not to want to resist in kind. However, to participate in violence, even in a moment of necessity, is to take the easy way out and give in to the fears and pressures of this broken world. It may be justified under some circumstances—self-defense or as a representative of the government—but to harm or kill does not put you on the "right side."

Violence is the result of the Fall, part of the arrival of sin and death into the world. Situations in the world make it necessary because the world is broken. But a complete commitment to pacifism would mean the end of any active resistance to evil by lawful governments.

There's a difference, however, between the actions a man might take as an agent of the government and what he must do as an ambassador of Christ. God ordained governments to protect their citizens (Romans 13:3–4), but He ordained His children to follow Christ, to love Him and others wholeheartedly, to seek peace, and to increase His kingdom (Romans 12:17–21).

Violence can't accomplish the ultimate purposes of God's

kingdom. We need to be the conscience of any movement, the ones who don't glorify violence as a means to God's ends. That's where we must turn the other cheek (Matthew 5:39–44), stand for the poor and oppressed, and love our enemies, all with non-violence. That's as radical a stance as anyone could ever take in this world.

Jesus, violence is part of this broken world. Because of that, I should never embrace it as something You support or justify—even if it is a necessity in certain situations. Let me not use Your Word and will to justify my behavior, but let me be guided by You in all I do. You died for all of us, and You don't want anyone to live apart from You. But You always give us the choice. And for me, even though I'm redeemed, You allow me to choose to seek You above all else. Let Your motives for interacting with people, for defending the weak and poor and helpless, be my motives.

• • •

Lord, the time is coming when I will suffer for following You (John 15:18), perhaps even violently. If it doesn't happen on a societal or global scale, it will happen on a personal level. Help me to face it the way Jesus did, looking to accomplish Your will before His own desire to avoid pain and suffering. He is my example: "For God called you to do good, even if it means suffering, just as Christ suffered for you" (1 Peter 2:21 NLT).

God, I acknowledge my own natural (that is, broken and sinful) tendencies toward violence. My heart has held onto bitterness, lust, anger, and greed, and harsh words have flowed from my mouth because of those things. These are all forms of violence. You warned Cain that if he didn't master his sinful desires, they would master him (Genesis 4:6–7). He didn't, and they did, to his great shame and his brother's death. Cleanse my heart of all iniquity.

. . .

Lord, when the blood of innocents cries out to me, it's hard not to at least think about a violent response. But You have said that vengeance is Yours, that You will repay wrongdoing (Hebrews 10:30). I want to obey You in serving the poor and oppressed, but I want to do it out of love, not out of anger and fear. If I must use violence to defend my family or to protect innocents in dangerous and unstable parts of the world, let me not justify it as Your perfect will but as a necessity in a broken world.

. . .

Father, You have called me to peace. Because You are my peace, and because You desire reconciliation with anyone who would come to You, I turn from pursuing even the thought of violence as a way to achieve justice. That's Your job. Violence is part of this fallen world, but it should never be anything but the last resort. I pray for those whose job it is to be peacemakers and law keepers, that You would give them wisdom and help them to build a greater sense of unity in our communities and world. Help me to be aware of anyone around me who might be hurting and looking to hurt others, and give me the courage and the words to reach out before they make a terrible decision.

WEAKNESS

In the same way, the Spirit helps us in our weakness.
We do not know what we ought to pray for, but the Spirit
himself intercedes for us through wordless groans.

ROMANS 8:26 NIV

• • •

It's hard for a man to admit that he feels weak. We men want to always at least give the appearance of being in control, of having the situation in hand, of being prepared for every contingency. But how realistic is that?

When you came to Christ, part of it involved acknowledging that you needed Him, that you could never overcome your sin on your own. And yet, that tendency to fall back on your own strength keeps popping up, compounded by the lie that if you were really growing in Christ, you would somehow know what to do in every situation and would therefore be able to handle hardship better.

Listen to Paul's thoughts about doing that: "This only I want to learn from you: Did you receive the Spirit by the works of the law, or by the hearing of faith? Are you so foolish? Having begun in the Spirit, are you now being made perfect by the flesh? Have you suffered so many things in vain—if indeed *it was* in vain?" (Galatians 3:2–4 NKJV).

By faith you received Christ, were saved, and received

the Holy Spirit. God permits the other battles that come along and wear you out to test that faith, to make sure you're still relying on Him and not falling back into the futility of your old self-sufficiency. If you're feeling worn out, there's always a possibility that it's because you've been trying to do everything on your own—something you already know won't work. You will always need God, and that's okay—it's good, in fact! Let Him be your strength.

God, I am worn out. So many things have been happening that require my care and attention, but somehow I let my busyness push my need for You out of the picture. It's no wonder I'm so frustrated and weak. But here I am, snapping out of it. I need You, Lord. Your grace is enough for me. I know You will give me what I need—the rest, the wisdom, the will—to keep seeking You as life rolls on.

. . .

Father, I spend so much time trying to decide which is the good, which is the better, and which is the best. I'm juggling too many things. I need Your discernment, Your wisdom, and Your perspective to determine what is best—that is, whatever You want me to do next. Teach me how to say no. Help me figure out what to let go of and what to hold on to. You know what's best for me and the people in my life.

Lord, when David wrote Psalm 102, he subtitled it "A Prayer of one afflicted, when he is faint and pours out his complaint before the LORD" (ESV). As I read it aloud, please accept it as my prayer too. I need You, and I know You won't let me down.

. . .

Jesus, I need Your help. It's hard to even describe everything I'm feeling. I'm overwhelmed, disappointed, exhausted, and anxious, but I give it all to You. Thank You that You are at God's right hand right now, interceding for me in prayer (Hebrews 7:25). Give me Your grace, and help me to extend it to others, especially to those who are part of the issues I'm facing.

WORRY

*"Come to me, all who labor and are
heavy laden, and I will give you rest."*
MATTHEW 11:28 ESV

· · ·

Worry is the cause of a thousand sleepless nights, but it doesn't limit itself to tossing and turning in bed. Worry ripples outward, revealing a heart that struggles to fully trust God. Habitual worriers get stuck in their own heads, and that's when they start doing real damage to themselves and to others. A worrying Christian makes for a poor witness to God's ability to meet our most essential needs: love, grace, and forgiveness.

When you start to worry, ask yourself: How is it that I can trust God to break the chains of sin, change my ultimate destination from hell to heaven, and give me eternal life, but I can't trust in Him to pay my bills, protect my kids, mend my damaged relationship, or help me to overcome an addiction? Jesus said, "People who don't know God and the way he works fuss over these things, but you know both God and how he works. Steep your life in God-reality, God-initiative, God-provisions. Don't worry about missing out. You'll find all your everyday human concerns will be met" (Matthew 6:32–33 MSG).

Jesus called people driven by worry, "You of little faith"

(v. 30 ESV). Worry tells God you think your circumstances are more powerful than He is. Faith helps you master your circumstances by placing them in God's hands.

God, my thoughts are a train wreck—car after car full of care after care, all banging into each other. I know a lot of it is relatively trivial, but the little things I worry about become bigger issues surrounding the decisions I've made or the people those decisions have affected. I'm calling time out and coming to You with all of it. You care about all the details of my life, and I'm counting on Your peace—which is far beyond my understanding—to keep my mind and thoughts on You and not on my worries (Philippians 4:6–7).

. . .

Jesus, remind me that You are not only with me but in me: "It is no longer I who live, but Christ lives in me. So I live in this earthly body by trusting in the Son of God, who loved me and gave himself for me" (Galatians 2:20 NLT). You didn't save me from the worst possible fate—eternal separation from God—just to leave me hanging on all these comparatively smaller details. You are my peace.

Lord, thank You for all You've done for me. You've blessed me with all I need, especially in my relationship with You in Christ. There's so much I can't control, but this is something I can do: seek You, thank You, praise You, and ask for Your help. Comfort me, Holy Spirit, and bring to mind all the things I need to recall right now about Your goodness and provision (John 14:26–27).

. . .

Father, You have not given me a spirit of fear, "but of power and of love and of a sound mind" (2 Timothy 1:7 NKJV). Worry is not from You, God, but from my fear and lack of faith. I will trust You because You are my God, and I know You love me. I humble myself under Your hand, knowing that You will lift me up in Your good timing. I trust Your Word: "Live carefree before God; he is most careful with you" (1 Peter 5:7 MSG).

SCRIPTURE INDEX

OLD TESTAMENT

NEW TESTAMENT